Do You Love Me or Am I Just Paranoid?

VILLARD / NEW YORK

Do You Love Me or Am I Just Paranoid?

THE SERIAL MONOGAMIST'S GUIDE TO LOVE

Carina Chocano

Library of Congress Cataloging-in-Publication data is available

ISBN 0-8129-9214-8

Villard Books website address: www.villard.com
Printed in the United States of America on acid-free paper
9 8 7 6 5 4 3 2
First Edition

Book design by Victoria Wong

For my dad,
who was fond of the expression
"To E.A.Ch. his own,"
because those were his initials

Oh, gallant was the first love, and glittering and fine;
The second love was water, in a clear white cup;
The third love was his, and the fourth was mine;
And after that, I always get them all mixed up.

—DOROTHY PARKER

Contents

Introduction

Despite the looming threat of repeated failure, people as a people are wildly optimistic about their prospects for love.

In fact, get enough drinks in them, and just before they try to hug you, a surprising number of people will confess to a heartfelt belief that love is all there is in this crazy, mixed-up slag heap of a world. While this belief is not entirely our fault, it's nothing to be proud of, either. Children who watch too much television harbor similar beliefs about sugary breakfast cereals, and we don't think them adorably romantic.

What is love, anyway, aside from a liquor-fueled period of psychosis counteracted with a lifetime's worth of received romantic notions and a tingling sensation in the pants? Of course, it's love's mysterious qualities that account for a large part of its enduring entertainment value. Most of us are attracted to rare and mysterious things, like truffles and Greta Garbo. Too much information is almost always a turnoff. (Note how "Foie Gras" sounds delightful, yet "Spreadable Ruptured Liver" does not.)

In fact, love is a nightmare of compromise and generosity. Still, when it goes wrong, when it fails to appear, or when it comes home blind drunk at three A.M. and pees on the bed, we experience disappointment and a crushing sense of failure. This causes many of us to suffer from what my mother (a picturesque foreigner) amusingly calls "low self-steam." We blame ourselves. We vow to embark on a vigorous self-improvement program the very next day. We may even purchase a self-help manual, or maybe a mug with an encouraging saying on it. But the path to self-improvement can be an expensive and hazardous row to hoe, assuming one would even want to hoe a row in the first place. Most of us, on consideration, would prefer not to.

In such a climate, it is not easy to talk about serial monogamy. For one thing, we don't have the words. Look up the word "relationship" in the thesaurus, and right away you'll see the problem. "Blood relation" doesn't do it, unless you have an attractive cousin and have decided to take advantage of recent changes in the law. "Connection" seems a weak and rather tepid alternative, given the highly volatile nature of this particular type of "connection." "Dating"—an antiquated word that refers to something people did in the fifties and stopped doing once it became okay to openly sleep around—doesn't describe it either. Relationships can begin as early as the first "date," even if that "date," as such, never takes place.

But where are the words for that thing that happens when you meet someone (say, in college or at your first job or through a friend), hang out for a few weeks, keep hanging out for a few more years, and move in together, making sure not to purchase any big-ticket items together without holding on to the receipts? And what box do you check on your insurance forms when you've been living with the same person for five years but still aren't sure you want to get married because there are some things you have to work on first? You know. Relationships. What's another word for them?

It may very well be a semantic problem. As words go, "relationship" is conveniently elastic, and can be used to describe any number of associations, connections, affiliations, dalliances, flings, flirtations, long- and short-term bonds. In almost every instance, it is used to describe ambivalent sexual liaisons that are neither legally binding nor particularly exciting. It is not known, exactly, when the word "relationship" came to replace other, more descriptive, terms like "courtship," "engagement," "marriage," "illicit extramarital love affair," and "rebound." Experts trace its modern usage back to a time when people were no longer forced to conduct their love affairs in private, but were still too embarrassed to use the word "lover" in public. Thankfully, this is still the case.

I do not claim to be an expert in the field of successful relationships. But if any subject lends itself to the sort of indolent, poorly researched, and whimsically half-cocked theories I will put forth in this mercifully slim volume, it's the practice of segueing from one committed relationship to another without pausing to consider why one is segueing from one committed relationship to another.

Is there advice contained in this book? Yes, but it's terrible. On the other hand, it's probably just the sort you generally give yourself, so there's no hard work involved. If you follow it, you will learn how to leap blindly from relationship to relationship, how to ignore your better instincts, how to drag out a doomed affair, how to enter into an exciting rebound, how to make the most of your ex-girlfriend persona, and more—just like you've been doing all along. The fact is that serial monogamy is now the norm. Consequently, there's no reason to keep looking upon it as some kind of repetitive failure pattern. Maybe we should just start regarding it as a flower pattern or paisley.

So, whether you're sticking it out in a halfhearted entanglement or jumping into the arms of the next emotional disaster to come along, just remember: whatever your justifi-cations for choosing "toxic," "dysfunctional," or just "long, difficult, and ultimately doomed" relationships over fun, sup-portive, carefree love romps, an unbroken string of failed relationships will not earn you frequent flier miles, but it is not without rewards.

The world is a treasure trove of possibility. Perhaps you will inherit a million dollars someday and spend your life traveling to far-flung, exotic locations. Until that happens, however, why not make the most of traveling to exotic emo-tional states and flinging yourself face-first on the bed? After all, if it weren't for so-called "bad" relationships, many of us would have no relationships at all.

Someday your prince will come. And if he doesn't, some other dude will. In the meantime, why not milk the drama for all it's worth?

PART ONE

The Monogamist's Way

Wash, Rinse, Repeat:
Serial Monogamy for Beginners

Love comes in all shapes and sizes. For some, it takes the form of a rhombus. For others, it appears in the shape of a comely goat or a total dick. But whatever its contours, we have all been conditioned over the years to believe that love must eventually assume the venerable marriage shape in order to best advertise its successful conclusion to others. And throughout the years, this notion has been brutally enforced by *The New York Times'* "Vows" section.*

And yet, popular as matrimony has become in recent years, interest in the lives of attractive single people—especially single people under forty who can pass for thirty, thirty-five, max; but never, ever the sad, fat kind—has become ever more prurient and frothy. Suddenly, the notion that single life is an uninterrupted orgy of indulgent "me-time"—if you can afford the right clothes and lots of beaded throw pillows and expensive toiletries—is being just as rigorously enforced as the idea that marriage is a never-ending love story. Dozens of publications are dedicated to tracking the spotty romantic careers of our most renowned and illustrious serial monoga-

---

* Personally, I am a big fan of the "Vows" section, as I am always interested to learn what the bride does for a living or where the groom's stepmother resides. I, for one, can't get enough of the meet-cute stories and the tasteful mention of prestigious alma maters. In fairness, the paper of record might consider a section celebrating unions of a more tentative kind. A "Shacking Up" section might be nice.

mists, but rarely will yet another Julia Roberts relationship meltdown inspire *People* magazine to run her photo with a headline that reads "Single and Hating It!" Why? Because if magazines and television shows are to be believed, being single and female is like a long, drunken day at Disneyland. And in the magic shoe kingdom, you don't walk the least bit funny in four-inch heels.

No wonder you feel bad. You are not technically married. You are not technically single. You have been leaping from one long, sincere, "committed" relationship to another like an overstimulated squirrel monkey. Sure, you have gone on dates—they just happen to have lasted three to five years. That's because, traditionally, you have started to worry about never finding love again within about twenty-four hours of the demise of your last relationship. Paradoxically, you have always found love again within twenty-four hours of starting to worry—a pattern you will likely repeat until undesirability sets in.

Are you a complete pudwhacker? Or are you onto something? While you may have other, perfectly good reasons to feel bad about yourself, don't let this one in particular get you down. No matter how culturally invalidated you may feel, there is nothing wrong with you, your tepid decisions, or your ambivalent approach to love and commitment. Think of it this way: it is quite possible that you have unconsciously devised a clever way to live the life of a married person and a single person *simultaneously* without cheating, lying, or developing a set of discrete personalities, each with its own hobbies and dietary restrictions. Why tie the knot, when you can simply leave the rope slung casually over your throat? Why be single on a Saturday night, when you can be single, and therefore trendy, on the dotted line? If nothing else, the experience of barreling through a series of committed relationships has probably made you the wiser and stronger beneficiary of an impressive collection of boxer shorts. And while these boxer shorts have probably come at an emotional price much higher than $16.99, the wisdom, the memories, the laughs, the holes punched in the wall— they have doubtless passed the time.

Still, there comes a time in every serial monogamist's life when someone—an uncle, perhaps, or a series of uncles, a mother, a few cousins, and a boss or two—asks the inevitable question: "Whatever happened to that other guy, what was his name? You know, the asshole?" Unnerving as this question can be, it's important to remember that at least you got out—which is more than you can say for Grandma.

So instead of dwelling on the negative, let's try a new approach and take a moment to reexamine the advantages of being a serial monogamist in today's uncertain world.

"Ambivalent" Doesn't Have to Mean "Alone"

Half-assed relationships have gained popularity in recent years, as they present the ideal romantic choice for people who dislike themselves and others equally, and yet cannot bear the thought of being alone. You have doubtless heard members of the psychiatric profession suggest, in their "soothing" voices, that we cannot expect to be loved by others if we do not love ourselves. And yet, if we truly loved ourselves, what need would we have for others? As Deepak Chopra once said, we do not strangle our own chickens, and yet we expect occasionally to dine at Kenny Rogers Roasters.

As we now understand them, relationships allow a couple to remain in a noncommittal monogamous union for an indeterminate period of time with no clear goal in mind, while simultaneously shielding them from the twin horrors of breaking up and getting married. (See also "Aging.")

All the Illusion of Options with None of the Scary Options

Do you have trouble making decisions? Are you resistant to change? If your relationship is beginning to chafe, but you find that the thought of starting all over again triggers an even more unsightly rash, emotional paralysis may be right for you. After all, not everyone is cut out to be an intrepid love-seeker. Perhaps you are more of the shy, trepid type. Maybe you are not as open to life's journeys as you are to life's quick errands. Remember that, at your center, you are a luminous jewel, and therefore fundamentally legless. Stay put, but let your imagination soar. Why risk the emotional Chernobyl that is a breakup, when you can simply envision it? Why invite fresh disappointments when your nagging doubt and confusion are so cozy and familiar? Remember, as long as it remains safely in your mind, your next relationship will be perfect.

It's Never Too Late to Start Over

There is nothing like the late stage of a moribund relationship to make a person feel like a half-dead whale flopping around on a deserted beach after everyone has gone home for the winter; and there is nothing like the sheer giddiness of the early stages of a relationship to transform that whale into a radiant Pamela Anderson–style figure, jogging in slow motion toward her glorious future. Luckily, relationships are nonbinding and therefore marvelously flexible. If you find that you have accidentally committed to the wrong person, you may scrap the commitment and commit again with total impunity. Even if, during the course of your last relationship, you rarely left the house, the two of you were still technically "dating," and therefore officially just passing through.

And Who's This Now?

Teddy and Louise have been together for a little under a year. Recently, they were invited to the wedding of one of Louise's cousins. Before going out with Teddy, Louise spent a year with a man named Daryl, whom the family had never liked much, but were just starting to get used to. Before that there was Chuck. Everybody loved Chuck. To this day, Louise's Noni talks about Chuck, sighing, "You had true love and you let it slip away!" Louise has never had the heart to tell her Noni that Chuck was a phone sex addict.

Anyway, Teddy and Louise arrived at the wedding to find that Teddy's place card had not only rechristened him "Freddy," but that they had invented a new last name for him entirely. Teddy and Louise considered correcting the mistake, but somehow never got around to it. They know what everybody's thinking: Another year, another boyfriend. Slut.

How to Be a Serial Monogamist

The best way to keep the boyfriends coming is to be devastatingly beautiful. If this is not within your budget, it is advisable to develop an attractive personality. While most people will agree on what makes a person devastatingly beautiful, many find it harder to reach a consensus about what makes for an attractive personality. These days, it's even harder to ascertain whether someone has a nice personality, or whether his or her doctor has achieved the perfect psychotropic cocktail. Don't be alarmed if you become involved with someone whose doctor is still experimenting.

Which leads to the good news: Thanks to the widespread availability of personality-enhancing chemicals and the vast army of personal gurus at our disposal, our personalities are changeable as the wind, maybe even more so. This is never more true than at the beginning of a new relationship.

Starting a relationship is a little like starting at a new school—nobody knows you were a social pariah known only as "Stinky Lip," and, more important, *nobody has to know.* As far as your new potential boyfriend goes, your class picture was never pasted to the urinal in the boys' bathroom, and you never spent any significant amount of time in the Dumpster behind the gym. It is permissible to eventually reveal the sordid details of your past, but only after your boyfriend has made it his personal mission to save you from yourself.

The realization that it is possible to reinvent oneself from scratch at the start of a new affair can be a heady one, and many ambitious young lovers find they don't know just where to begin. Follow these basic approaches to get started:

1. Adaptive

The adaptive monogamist tailors her personality to the tastes of the person she is currently seeing. This is an evolutionary trait that has aided countless invertebrate species in the art of continued survival. Before approaching her target, the adaptive monogamist makes a careful study of his behaviors, preferences, beliefs, and habits. She then methodically alters her own to suit, taking great care to simulate a long-term interest and devotion to his hobbies and personal causes. Should the monogamist's efforts to transform herself into the woman of her love-object's dreams be discovered by friends, roommates, or family members, she should claim total ignorance regarding the matter. It is perfectly admissible to completely alter one's musical tastes, for example, as long as one is steadfast in denying that such a transformation is taking place. While some may find this sort of behavior distasteful and dishonest, it should be pointed out that the adaptive monogamist's old behaviors, etc., are actually those of her ex-boyfriend. In other words, she is not really changing into someone else. She is simply molting.*

* A word of caution: If you are very young or pathologically insecure, you may be laboring under the misapprehension that the best way to convince your new love of your depth of feeling is by copying his tastes in everything. While it is always nice to share some interests with your beloved, sudden, unforeseen vegetarianism is not becoming in anyone. Neither are unexpected conversions to R&B, heroin, Jerry Lewis pictures, motorcycle

2. Passive-Aggressive

The passive-aggressive monogamist knows that nothing attracts a boyfriend like dysfunction, and therefore seeks to highlight her own shortcomings in an attempt to pass them off as a sort of fascinating complexity. Blindsided by her rampant displays of selfishness/bitchiness/immaturity, the new boyfriend will find himself strangely compelled to fix her problems. Depending on the complexity and depth of these problems, they should keep the relationship fueled for anywhere from one to three years, after which point the passive-aggressive monogamist will herself come to be viewed as the problem.

3. Reactive

The reactive monogamist knows exactly what she wants in a boyfriend: the exact opposite of her last boyfriend. Unfortunately, this often means trading good qualities for bad ones, then doing it again, then again. Eventually, chances are good that the reactive monogamist will come full circle, become very dizzy, and have to sit down.

4. Sarcastic

The sarcastic monogamist knows how to charm the pants right off prospective boyfriends by passing her bad attitude off as a withering sense of humor. Once pants have been re-

---

leather, or The Forum. Unless you want to alienate everyone who knew you before last week, please make an effort to "try new things" in moderation. While imitation is the sincerest form of flattery, it is also unimaginably creepy.

moved, however, this approach loses effectiveness. It is the rare naked person who appreciates the fruits of a caustic wit.

Other popular personalities to consider:

- ♥ Vixen
- ♥ One of the guys™
- ♥ Low-maintenance
- ♥ Lacto-vegetarian

Bend Over: Assuming the Position of Compromise

As with most things in life, relationships are a series of compromises. If you find it easy to compromise your desires, your ideals, and your judgment, you're well on your way.

Step 1: Lower Your Standards

A general rule of thumb when it comes to looking for love in the modern world is to stop being so picky. If you include your nightmares, the person of your dreams is within your reach. Once you've expanded your horizons to include people you formerly deemed "unacceptable," including bosses, therapists, spiritual and political leaders, sworn enemies, and distant cousins, you'll find a whole universe opening up to you and you'll be well on your way to a series of delightful adventures, unexpected surprises, and astonishing displays of bizarre behavior. If you've already done this, do it again. You'll be amazed at the sheer number of unsuitable matches to be made right in your neighborhood.

Start by asking yourself the following:

- Does he really have to be attractive?
- Does he really have to be smart?
- Does he really have to be financially secure?
- Does he really have to be funny?

- Does he really have to be clean?
- Does he really have to be sane?

Step 2: Question Your Instincts

Your gut is telling you to run far away. Pretend not to hear it. If it insists, pretend not to speak gut. Conveniently store your better judgment under the bed until next needed, usually when the relationship starts to sour.

Step 3: Accentuate the Positive

Don't get bogged down in your negative emotions and judgments, as negativity may obscure a potential boyfriend's boyfriend potential. Before dismissing someone as "ugly" or "crazy," take the time to examine his positive qualities:

- Is he wonderfully weird?
- Is he thrillingly obsessive-compulsive?
- Is he expertly medicated?
- Is he relaxingly boring?
- Is he delightfully clueless?
- Is he charmingly vain?
- Is he adorably childlike and helpless?

Step 4: Adjust Your Mental Image

It is important to avoid formulating any sort of mental image of an ideal mate, as this may prevent you from falling for the first person to come along. Having nothing to compare actual partners to, your standards will be more malleable, and with any luck will evaporate entirely.

Step 5: Keeping the Ball Rolling

In Mandarin, the word for "I want your things out of here by tomorrow morning" is the same as the word for "opportunity." A true serial monogamist never looks upon a breakup as an end, but rather as a shiny new beginning. She also plans in advance whenever possible. Below are some tips from the pros.

The Marathon

However exhausting and emotionally draining, dragging out a doomed liaison does have its advantages. It provides an excellent excuse for shirking actual paying work in order to "work on the relationship" and is useful in helping to extract large quantities of attention from family and friends in the form of meals, interim lodging, tea, and pity. Also, drawing out an inevitable breakup over a period of several years is an excellent way to avoid being single. In order for this method to work, your partner must be as insecure and dysfunctional as you are. How can you tell if your partner is in it for the long—but not permanent—haul? Various behaviors can tip you off, including a willingness to enter couples counseling in order to gain an ally and the habit of making popcorn at the beginning of each argument.

The Relay

Some people prefer to seek out their next relationship while securely ensconced in the old one. This is not unlike going out to lunch right after breakfast, just in case locusts decimate the crops. Because this practice is generally frowned upon, it is recommended that you display some serious agony over the shift. Explain that your new affair "just happened," despite your best efforts to the contrary. No one will believe you, but you should never admit the truth until your new boyfriend has become a permanent fixture at family functions and your old boyfriend is nothing more than a hazy memory. Once your old boyfriend has been forgotten by your friends and family, you can laugh about the whole crazy situation, coming across as adorably madcap and romantic. Everybody loves adorable madcap romantics, especially when the adorable madcap romantics' ex-boyfriends keep calling them in tears, searching for answers.

The Sprint

If the prospect of looking for a new relationship from the security of your old relationship makes you queasy, you might consider sprinting. Sprinters dash from one relationship straight into the next without so much as a backward glance. Sprinting has none of the ethical disadvantages of the Relay, while yielding similar results. On the downside, sprinters have less time to do their homework on new lovers, leading them to form dubious commitments very quickly. On the upside, arranged marriages aren't usually preceded by long getting-to-know-you periods, either, and they are proven to last longer and be more satisfying. Furthermore, sprinters will find that they can easily shift into marathon mode when the relationship begins to go south.

Your Romantic Career
(Formerly Your Checkered Past)

Serial monogamy, like any skill, is best learned in steps. One must walk before one can run. Similarly, one must learn to pull someone's hair before one can accuse someone of emotional unavailability. A true serial monogamist understands the importance of paying dues early in life, as she may not get the chance to later in this, our youth-obsessed culture.

The Formative Years

Very young people have an innate sense of caution when it comes to forming long-lasting alliances with members of the opposite sex. This is a basic survival skill usually learned early. But thanks, in part, to the popularity of television shows aimed at the precocious teen, tween, and zygote demographic, more and more children have begun to enter into long-term monogamous relationships with other immature people, long before necessary.

Elementary School: In elementary school, "going out" consists of not going anywhere and barely speaking to one another. If there is any sexual contact involved, it is tentative, awkward, and usually leads directly to a wordless parting of ways and vague feelings of hostility. It is, in other words, excellent training for future interactions.

Middle School: Middle school children are not, as a rule, attractive or fun to be around. Sadly, love-feelings are perhaps at their most intense during middle school. Hormones begin to kick in, intensifying unwarranted crushes while heightening fear of humiliation. In order to make up for this imbalance, middle school children tend to reserve their ardor for pop icons, movie stars, popular kids, and other unattainable types. This process is effective in introducing the little ones to love's spin-off emotions: depression, bitterness, and despair.

High School: Many kids—especially the slutty ones—reach high school feeling exhausted and disillusioned. This may lead them to form attachments hastily and adhere to them for excessively long periods of time. Teens who emulate married couples during their high school days will often find themselves beset by the desire to make out with people in 7-Eleven parking lots as they approach middle age. As this type of behavior can have serious legal ramifications, becoming "serious" in high school is not recommended. Conversely, teens who were not so lucky in high school love will often approach relationships later in life with the sort of get-it-while-you-can famine mentality that can lead to stomach rupture.

College: College is a fork in the road, relationship-wise. Patterns begin to emerge. Some people take a practical approach to dating, seeking out partners with sensible majors like economics and binge-drinking, whereas others begin tunneling blindly through a complex labyrinth of "artistic," "smart," or "unique" lovers. Whether you choose to get on the expressway to marriage or impale yourself on the prongs of bohemian love-torment is up to you.

Thank You for Choosing Bohemian Love-Torment!! (Special Advertising Section)

Thank you for choosing bohemian love-torment! We realize you have many choices when planning your romantic future, and we appreciate your placing your trust in us!! Just tell us what you have in mind and let us hammer out the details. Dreaming of a private squabble somewhere very public? We can handle that! Or maybe you're picturing the two of you in scenic Hawaii, contemplating the Pacific Ocean at sunset. Can you hear the trade winds? That's because you haven't spoken to each other in days! Slightly insecure, a little peeved, a tad confused, or out of your mind with jealousy—whatever your vision, we can make it happen!!

Choose from one of our most popular packages, and let us cater to all your psychosexual needs!!!!!!

Psychotic Splendor

Imagine yourself careening gaily through a series of safe relationships with dull, plain, or otherwise ineffectual people you know will never leave you. The warm breeze of security envelops you, as you look out onto a majestic tropical garden and wonder what you are doing here. Sudden mood swings by candlelight, despair at dusk. Is this all there is?

(Poolside breakfast, butterfly or dove release, escape hatch. $350 inclusive.)

Traumatizing Memories

Addicted to surprise? You've heard all the horror stories, now live them for yourself! Sudden, unforeseen betrayal doesn't just have to be something that happens to other people! Walk in on your boyfriend in a compromising position with a delivery person, come home from work to find the furniture gone, meet your husband's other wife at the hair salon. Getting dumped was never so memorable.

(Professional photographer, therapist on call. $475 inclusive.)

Sunset Threnody

Whisper your regrets against a scarlet-gold sunset. Listen to the repetitive rhythm of the ocean surf—is it beckoning you? Is it trying to tell you something? Like "Run far away"? Don't forget to take the stereo!

(Signature floral arrangements, cocktails and canapés, getaway limo. $415 inclusive.)

All of our bohemian love-torment packages can be customized to suit your needs. Some optional extras include promised phone calls that never come, awkward silences, vastly different expectations, tragic misunderstandings, and VD. We're here to make it memorable! But don't just take our word for it, listen to what our satisfied clients have to say about us!!

> "Thanks to Bohemian Love-Torment, my life is the engine of torture I always dreamed it could be."
> —Doreen del Olmo, Evanston, IL

"I've been dating musicians since I was sixteen. Now that I'm thirty-seven and living with a drummer, I can't believe what I was thinking! I never in my wildest dreams imagined my life would turn out like this!"

—Dani Vasconcellos, Chicago, IL

"People often compliment me on my funny stories of loss and humiliation. I tell them all the credit should go to Bohemian Love-Torment!!!"

—Jamie Pelletier, San Francisco, CA

"You've made my life hell!"

—Kiki Schwartztrauber, New York, NY

PART TWO

You and
Your Precious
Feelings

Going Through the Emotions

As your failed relationships pile up behind you, so certain emotions will accumulate and fester in your tender psyche. Do not reject your bad feelings. As an adventuresome traveler on the path to love, you are open to whatever gifts come your way, even if you decide to return them later. Cherish your feelings and make them feel welcome. Invite them in, ask them about their day, inquire as to whether they would like a Fig Newton. If they decline, insist, as perhaps they are just being polite.

The world is full of people who would like to tell you to relax, calm down, chill out, go away, and please, please, please just shut up for once. Do not heed their siren call. Tie yourself to the mast of your emotions. Remember, feelings have feelings, too. And nothing hurts them more than being ignored.

When casting a backward glance over relationships gone by, it is important to remember that, no matter how disappointing, alarming, baffling, or expensive, they have not been entirely without value. While it is true that so-called "healthy" relationships are generally less taxing than terminal ones, they also tend to breed a certain kind of pudding-faced complacency that may annoy and alienate those less fortunate. A challenging relationship, on the other hand, forges the spirit, quickens the pulse, and sets the mind—and sometimes the curtains—on fire. Do not, for instance, underestimate the character-building effects of "not being heard." Feeling chronically misunderstood is an excellent way to hone and polish your hair-trigger responses to perceived rejection. Once you have amassed a suitable automatic defensive posture for every occasion, you will have more time to dedicate to pursuits more interesting than listening to what someone has to say about you. It is a sad fact of life that what someone has to say about you is rarely pleasant. Similarly, relationships in which trust is an issue are helpful in developing the imagination. Resentment has been known to sharpen the wit. Anger can add to one's air of mystery. Above all, keep in mind that whatever the set of colorful neuroses you have collected in the course of your romantic life, they are *your* colorful neuroses. And as the noted serial monogamist Gustave Flaubert once said, our bad relationships, *sont nous.*

When Thinking Too Much
Is Not Enough

Thinking is the spice of life. Without thoughts, we might be reduced to spending our days mechanically accomplishing things without taking time to obsess about the roses. Where would be the joy?

While it's true that focused, educated thinking—when applied to practical problems—has been known to help people solve complicated mathematical equations, invent useful appliances, and decide what to wear, aimless, unfocused thoughts are integral to our quality of life. Left to ricochet freely between cranial walls, thoughts tend to go haywire, providing an excellent way to add emotional conflict to an otherwise monotonous existence.

Contrast the relative dullness of an unexamined life to that of a life examined within an inch of itself:

Life, Unexamined:

7:00 A.M.—Wake up, quickly rise from bed
7:04 A.M.—Enjoy brisk shower
7:15 A.M.—Select appropriate outfit
7:30 A.M.—Drive to work
8:00 A.M. to 6:00 P.M.—Work
6:10 P.M.—Drive home
7:00 P.M.—Eat sensible dinner

7:00 to 10:00 P.M.—Gaze peacefully at TV, boyfriend, or wall
10:15 P.M.—Sleep

Life, Intensely Scrutinized:

7:00 A.M.—Wake up. Wonder why. Demand to know why
you weren't born to a life of unimaginable wealth and
idleness. Realize there is no one there to answer you.
Blame father for appalling state of affairs. Fall asleep.

8:00 A.M.—Wake up again. Contemplate day ahead. Grow
unaccountably depressed.

8:30 A.M.—Decide to skip shower as showering ultimately
futile, Sisyphean task. Curse system that demands such
impossible hygienic standards from creative free spirits.
Liberally apply deodorant and consider business done.

8:30 to 9:15 A.M.—Rummage through closet. Try on things
that don't fit. Hate self for buying saris, jodhpurs, corsets,
slutty party dresses, and too-tight pants instead of sensible
items one might wear in public. Wonder what's in fridge.

9:30 A.M.—Drive to work. Practice excuses for tardiness.
Imagine boss not buying excuses for tardiness. Focus on
boss's bad qualities. Hate boss. Note stringy hair and unpleasant sensation in armpits.

10:00 A.M. to 6:00 P.M.—Pretend to work while methodically
cataloguing everything that is wrong with life. Wonder
why one hasn't showered. Wonder why one never learns.
Regret that one was not born to life of brilliance and effi-
ciency. Blame mother for appalling state of affairs.

6:10 P.M.—Drive home, thinking about how life has become
increasingly monotonous and senseless. Blame friends.

7:00 P.M.—Rummage through refrigerator. Eat crackers. Eat
cereal. Blame self for not going grocery shopping. Reconsider and blame boss.

7:14 P.M.—Wonder why crush hasn't called.

7:15 to 7:16 P.M.—Wonder if perhaps crush is not wondering same. Pick up phone.

7:16 to 7:17 P.M.—Reconsider. Put phone down.

7:17 to 7:18 P.M.—Wonder if perhaps expecting crush to call is retro excuse for passivity and inability to take charge of own life. Pick up phone.

7:18 to 7:19 P.M.—Realize that if crush wanted to talk, he would call. Put phone down.

7:19 to 7:21 P.M.—Concentrate on not calling. Repeat mindless mantra to self to aid in not calling.

7:22 P.M.—Pick up phone and dial. Wait for answering machine to pick up. Hang up.

7:23 P.M.—Become terrified at prospect that crush has caller ID. Hate crush. Blame the phone company.

7:23 to 10:00 P.M.—Replay scenario in which crush is screening calls in order to deliberately avoid self's call over and over again in head. Begin feeling woozy.

2:15 A.M.—Pass out due to vertiginous drop in blood sugar level.

Are You My Future?

Susan and Tony think the world of each other. The problem is that, sometimes, when they look at each other, they wonder if perhaps they could do better. Have they settled for less than they deserve? Do people wonder what they are doing together? Is it possible they don't quite realize how good-looking they are? That's what everybody always tells them.

Sometimes, when they think about this, one of them asks the other, "What are you thinking about?" And the other one says, "Nothing." And they hug and laugh and start to kiss.

What to Read into Virtually Every Situation

Overthinking is a great way to turn a nonrelationship into a long, drawn-out, unrequited attachment with serious dramatic potential. In the beginning, it is important to overthink even the tiniest details. Plumb the secret language of silence for hidden clues to his innermost thoughts. What does his absence really mean? Does "I'll call you" always mean "I'll call you"? Or can it mean "I have to go"?

When overthinking, throw out outmoded ideas about what "a person who likes you" "would" or "should" do under "normal" circumstances. Remember, the object of your obsession is not just a "friend" or "person." The "normal" rules don't apply. The reasons for your love interest's failure to call are always deep, meaningful, and significant. It is important to meditate on the reasons he is not calling. Did you blow it by being too "available," too "nice," or "yourself"?

On the other hand, there is always the possibility that the power of your connection and the sheer wattage of electricity generated between you has overwhelmed him, causing him to retreat for fear of losing himself in the madness. Maybe he is not calling because he is afraid of letting you know how much he cares. Maybe he is seeing somebody else. Does he love you? Does he hate you? Does he remember meeting you? These are very good questions, and ones that cannot be asked enough.

Never let a simple exchange go by without running it through the wringer of your neuroses in search of possible clues. For example, consider the following conversation:

HIM: Hi.
YOU: Hi.

HIM: So, how are you?
YOU: Great.
HIM: Great.
YOU: You?
HIM: Great.
YOU: Great.
HIM: We should get together sometime.
YOU: That would be great.
HIM: I'll call you.

Clearly, the above exchange is rife with meaning and possibility. It may also contain one or more of the following: thinly disguised innuendos, double entendres, existential questions, cries for help, desperate attempts to be heard above the din of humanity, death threats, coded messages, cruel taunts, a riddle, the meaning of life, risqué allusions, declarations of undying love, malicious slander, a thread of hope, reasons to worry, and compelling but unconfirmed rumors. Given all the possible interpretations, how should you construe the above exchange?

First, commit it to memory. This is an important first step, as, in order to figure it out, you will be called upon to repeat it in your head over and over again. Next, pick yourself off the sofa and phone your best friend. Describe the exchange in excruciating detail. If your friend is at all skilled in these matters, she should home in on three tiny but very important details. They are:

A. That "So"

The first clue that there is more to this exchange than meets the ear. Were it not for that "so," the question could be easily dismissed as a simple inquiry into the state of your health or general well-being. But the "so" throws the whole thing off balance. What does it mean?

First, check the inflection. A versatile little syllable, "so" can pack a good deal of flirtatiousness; it can also drip with contempt or condescension. Try to recall the accompanying facial expression. Was your beloved smiling? Grave? Sneering? Addressing someone else? Second, try and remember what happened the last time you saw each other. Did you manage to pass yourself off as a reasonably poised individual? Or did you wind up with your elbow in the guacamole? Be honest with yourself. It will save you valuable time and energy. The thrill of "I'll call you" can be a heady one. It can also be a cheesy one.

B. Oh, Should We?

What does "We should get together sometime" really mean? It depends entirely on who is suggesting the outing. If the person saying it is a friendly girl who shares your interest in dog-breeding, then it means "We should get together sometime." Otherwise, it can mean anything from "I may give you a ring on a slow night" to "You're boring me." Whatever it means, it's probably not "I'm falling helplessly in love with you." Sadly, this is the interpretation you will choose to go with, simply because he said,

C. I'll Call You

"I'll call you" can be a particularly problematic phrase, as it carries with it the distinct whiff of promise. More often, what you are smelling is the tangy waft of a fetid lie. It's not necessarily that he does not intend to call, it's that people who say "I'll call you" tend to say it to a lot of people, and may fail to remember who "you" are once you are no longer in their direct line of vision. People who intend to call say things like "What's your number?" People who say "I'll call you" just like to hear the way it sounds. In their defense, it is entirely possible that they spent their entire high school careers coated in Clearasil, waiting for the day when they, too, could utter that magical phrase and leave someone hanging.

Acting Out

✿ It is an abiding fact of the serial monogamist's life that at some point or another, she will be labeled a "drama queen." Though such a characterization is almost never intended to be kind, you might as well make the most of it.

The serial monogamist is naturally drawn to drama and possesses an uncanny flair for showmanship. Often, she is at the center of a burlesque of her own devising. Her knack for histrionics, combined with her natural theatricality, quite often result in stunning *coups de théâtre* as are rarely seen on stage or screen.

Your experience as a drama queen will come in especially handy in the weeks and months following the demise of your last serious relationship. Take advantage of the ensuing emotional roller-coaster ride by thinking of your life as a movie. Cast yourself in the title role, and emote shamelessly and prodigiously in public. It's no accident that our friends in the theater and our friends crying themselves to sleep again in the spare room are often one and the same. After all, they cannot be held accountable for emotions that they are only borrowing for the time being. Our thespian brethren have much to teach us in the ways of high-strung love. For example, the next time you want to dump someone because you already have your eye on someone else, try saying something like "I just don't think I know what love *is*," in a dramatic whisper, with a straight face. As long as your life has become a soap opera, you might as well have an audience.

In fact, why not take your show on the road and . . .

CRINGE! as happily married ex-boyfriends express concern for your future happiness!

RECOIL! in horror as "old buddies" crawl out of the woodwork to buy you a drink within days of the demise of your last relationship!

MARVEL! at what the dates they set you up with reveal about what your friends really think of you!

REGALE! your friends with hilarious, gin-fueled tirades and tales of blind dates gone horribly, terrifyingly, and humiliatingly wrong!

It's Not Just a Pathology, It's a Lifestyle

We all know a happily married couple or two who just want to ruin things for the rest of us.*

The advantages of rejecting the happily married couple model ad hoc cannot be overstated. If you harbor even a whiff of doubt as to your chances of finding everlasting true love, happiness, connubial bliss, etc., etc., you would be wise to airily voice your rejection of it at every possible opportunity. This way, you may be unhappy forever, but at least you'll never be wrong.

Still, there will be times when you look upon your "happy" friends' smug union, then glance at your own shaky liaisons, then sneak another peek at their infernal contentment, then cast a hairy eyeball upon your own domestic arrangement, with its "rules" about "who" pays for "what" and "how much" you "owe me" and "where" is this relationship "going," and you will just want to throw in the towel and start all over again.

Just remember, your serial monogamy is not a reflection of your poor judgment or punishing personality. Think of it

---

*What exactly constitutes a happy couple is not entirely clear, as most ostentatiously happy couples are usually happier in front of others than in private. Don't be fooled, for example, by couples who make out in public. This type of behavior is not so much an expression of their love for each other as it is a sort of performance art personal ad. Nobody who puts that much energy into appearing happy can have any left over for anything else.

as a viable lifestyle choice that you have made, embraced, and engendered. You, after all, are the master of your destiny, at least occasionally. The sooner you accept that you have made this choice with wide-open eyes, the happier you will be.

A string of failed relationships is not a badge of shame. It is not a badge at all. It is a string of honor.

Serial Monogamy at a Glance

	Lifestyle Goal A: Monogamy	Lifestyle Goal B: Serial Monogamy
Primary Purpose	To meet and fall in love with your future mate.	To meet and fall in love with the first person to come along, in order not to have to go on any more dates for at least a few years.
Commonly Engaged in Activities	Any of a series of expensive, quasi-fun activities that require showering and leaving the house. Popular activities include: dinner at a nice restaurant, subtitled foreign films, fancy martini drinks at a trendy bar, Friday night jazz at the MoMA.	Any of a series of cheap, quasi-fun activities that do not require showering or leaving the house. Popular activities include: take-out on the couch, pop-up video on VH1, sharing a can of beer, never setting foot in the MoMA again.
Expected Protocol	Charming, flirtatious getting-to-know-you conversations punctuated by delighted squeals of laughter and modest yet secure presentation of one's personality.	Angry, resentful getting-to-know-you conversations punctuated by frustrated howls of pain and demanding yet pathetic laundry list of emotional needs.
Expected Results	Love	Love
Common Illusions	Love	Love

	Lifestyle Goal A: Monogamy	Lifestyle Goal B: Serial Monogamy
Common Misconceptions	That this charming, attractive, successful person would mirror, if yours, all of your best qualities.	That this boorish, dull, incredibly obtuse person is to blame for all of your worst qualities.
Secret Fears	That he or she will glean how much you like them and vanish.	That he or she will discover how much you hate them and vanish.
Usual Outcome	He or she gleans how much you like them and vanishes.	He or she discovers how much you hate them and wants to discuss it further.

Ever Closer

After having dated each other seriously for five years, Randy and Desiree have decided to take up residence on the same street. Desiree decided that being a mere block away from Randy more than made up for the hour added to her daily commute. "Randy wasn't sure that we knew each other well enough to move in together," Desiree says. "And it's true that with our work schedules, our relationship was perhaps not progressing as quickly as it would have if we were a couple of unemployed losers with nothing better to do."

Desiree spotted the charming one-bedroom bungalow one morning on her way to work. "It was four A.M., so I was a little bleary-eyed. At first I couldn't tell what it was, then I realized it was a 'For Rent' sign and I thought, 'That's it! I'll just home in on the fucker!'" Randy is delighted with the move, saying, "I was thinking about ending the relationship, because the drive to her place was a bitch and she wouldn't stop complaining about me not coming over more often. Now that I can just zip down the block at midnight and be back home in bed by one-thirty, two A.M., latest, it's made a big difference in my life."

PART THREE

Swingle!

That Single Feeling

The modern world is hell on single people. The ancient world was hell on single people, too, though few ever found this out. What with being betrothed to the leathery goatherd of their families' choice, exchanging livestock, hoeing vigorously, and dying soon afterward, they were usually too busy to look into it. Yes, perhaps they looked back on the carefree time before they married as the best eleven years of their entire lives. Or maybe they yearned for a day when people would be free to select their own mates, with no regard to goat-ownership, and walk out on them when the mood struck. Did they daydream, as they fished sheep pellets out of the milk bucket, of sexy weekend getaways at an exotic Sandals resort? We will never know.

What we do know is that being single today has very little to do with romantic weekend getaways, and a lot to do with doubt, fear, panic, insecurity, self-loathing, boredom, frustration, and mewling on the phone to anyone who will listen. After exhibiting these behaviors, people will assume we are single for a reason, and they will often assume correctly. The good news is, if you're single, you're not crazy. The questions you are asking yourself are valid and excellent. Are you unlovable? Dull? A little on the ugly side? Might your ass be mistaken for a crosstown bus on a badly lighted street corner? Only you can determine this, preferably late at night while waiting for the phone to ring.

Now that our parents have traded in the responsibility of choosing our partners for the responsibility of disapproving of them in retrospect, we are theoretically free to pick a mate from a selection of roughly six billion total strangers. This theory, while fabulous-sounding, is about as sound as the average Republican-sponsored education bill. In truth, few of us ever really have the chance to "select" our partners from a tempting assortment of people. The world is not your personal Whitman's Sampler—unless, of course, you have something everybody wants, like great big boobs or a great big trust fund, in which case the world *is* your personal Whitman's Sampler. (Congratulations!)

Those who have not been fantastically endowed either genetically or financially by their parents understand that we will not spend our lives lounging, metaphorically speaking, on a velvet chaise poking holes in bonbons until we find one we really like. More often, we will feel as though we have just had a hole poked in us before being discarded for a tantalizing coconut cream. And for once, our feelings will be onto something. Ultimately, when it comes to finding love, the grass will always be browner where you are sitting, mainly because it will lack sufficient oxygen and sunlight.

Singlehood and You

Maybe you are languishing in a monogamous relationship, toying with the idea of taking the leap into the yawning chasm of single life. Or you have already made the leap and are about to land in the outstretched arms of someone new. Naturally, you want to make sure to avoid mistakes. Any decision you make at this critical juncture will factor heavily in your future happiness, or at least in your happiness over the next two weeks, which could feel like forever. Meanwhile, you keep hearing things about the advantages of taking a long break between lovers. Friends begin to suggest that you consider "taking some time" to "focus on yourself," "reevaluate your priorities" and "heal."

Should you listen?

First, ask yourself who is doling out the advice. Chances are these people fall into one of three categories: single people who don't have your many opportunities and would sooner eat their own livers than see you fall in love again, single people in desperate need of other lonely single people to fill up their free time, and miserable couples with a stake in your unhappiness. Angrily reject their guidance, taking the opportunity to list their many failings in the arena of love and romance. Be sure to point out to them they are just jealous, as they may not be aware of it.

Next, try to determine whether you have the skills it takes to be single. Not everyone is equipped to handle the arduous task of tending to themselves without any outside assistance. Can you reach all the high places in your apartment? Are you handy with a drill? Do you take life's little obstacles in stride, or do you crumble in the face of adversity? At parties, are you skilled at looking people in the eye and enunciating clearly? Or do you have a tendency to drink until you cry? Do you enjoy exciting hobbies like mountain biking, kayaking, and volunteering? Or do you prefer to spend Sunday afternoons curled up on the bath mat, getting angry all over again about the time your dad gave you an eleven P.M. curfew on prom night?

It is important that you answer these questions honestly before taking the big step into single life. The decision to become single is not a step to be taken lightly, as it can lead to all sorts of problems that could become serious down the road. Try to picture yourself, single, at a variety of functions such as siblings' weddings, high school reunions, and your own funeral. Do you like what you see? In your mind's eye, are you interacting graciously with others, with no regard to their availability? Or are you glued to the buffet table, interacting with the cheese selection? Do you look okay? What are you wearing?

If the images that have just run through your head give you pause, perhaps you should reconsider "taking that time for yourself." Let's be honest, you're lucky that anyone wants to take that time away from yourself in the first place. No matter how trying the company of your current partner, it is important to remember that your own company, undiluted, may be even more loathsome.

It Didn't Work Out

Amanda is twenty-seven and had never had a serious boyfriend before. It isn't that she never meets anyone, it's just that she knows exactly what she is looking for in a guy and none of them matches her description. For example, she knows that her boyfriend will always open the car door for her and walk her to her door, which is why it didn't work out with Bruce. She also knows that her boyfriend will always call her several days in advance to make a date, which is why it didn't work out with Ken. One thing she doesn't know is that Ken's roommate decided to throw himself a birthday party at the last minute, so Ken could not possibly have called her in advance. Nor does she know that Ken has no idea why she's being such a bitch. Which is really why it didn't work out with Ken.

Where to Meet: Spinning
Your Wheels Successfully

The first few weeks following a breakup are a time of high hopes and higher expectations. The postbreakup euphoria period is often characterized by a desire to create the social life you have neglected over the course of a long, contentious relationship.

The issue of where to meet new people to fall in love with has been explored in some depth by the 200 million dating experts practicing in the United States today, and the sum of their knowledge can be coalesced into one inscrutable nut of advice, namely "Singles Events." What is a "Singles Event"? Nobody knows. Except for the 200 million dating experts practicing in the United States today, no one has ever attended one. We can only conclude from this that "singles event" is dating expert jargon for "whorehouse" or "Laundromat."

In order to properly address the issue of where to meet people who might be interested in spending a few years with you, some dangerous myths about finding love in the big city should first be dispelled.

Big-City Love Lie #1: Bigger Pond, More Fish

Buoyed by a sense of limitless possibility, many people move to big cities early in their romantic careers. In theory, such a move should increase our chances of finding the right person. In practice, it usually just increases our chances of finding more of the wrong ones. Though perhaps appealing as an idea, the actual work of trying to select a mate from a large sampling of humanity is as exhausting as it is ultimately unrewarding. As many of us have learned the hard way, population density is not a factor in luck-in-love. This is why BEIJING IS FOR LOVERS bumper stickers are relatively rare.

Big-City Love Lie #2: Bigger Pond, Smaller Splash

City life rarely offers the anonymity it's known for. In fact, big-city gossip is just small town gossip with publicists. While you may think you are conducting your affairs with the discretion of a Freemason, news of your exploits will get around. This is one of modern life's great paradoxes: the larger the dating pool, the more suspiciously warm the water.

Big-City Love Lie #3: More Fish, Better Odds

Big cities are cutthroat and competitive. This goes for finding jobs, housing, tables at restaurants, and dates. While few people expect to find the apartment of their dreams at bargain-basement prices, they are horrified to realize that some of the same principles apply to human interaction. This is why it's important to adjust your expectations, just as you would when looking for a place to live. No matter how long you look, you will probably wind up in a dwelling that is small, ugly, stifling, and expensive. The same principle applies to relationships. The main difference is that while, where apartments are concerned, you get what you pay for, with relationships, you eventually pay for what you get.

It should come as no surprise, then, when big-city life fails to yield the results you crave. But where, then, should you look?

Begin by searching your apartment. While at first this may seem fruitless, you really never know. Is the cable guy there? Maybe you recently ordered a pizza. A clean sweep of your dwelling is a necessary first step, as you never know when you'll run into an old flame, just sitting there, on the couch, watching basketball.

If your apartment yields nothing, don't be discouraged. Simply go outside and take a walk. Meeting people is all about having the right attitude. The sooner you adjust yours, the sooner you'll realize that the world is full of people reaching out, trying to make your acquaintance. What about that nice man huddled in the doorway, asking you for spare change and a smile? Like he says, it can't be that bad! Or what about those roofers over there? They sure seem friendly. And they're obviously not afraid to communicate their needs.

If the people you meet on the street are not to your liking, try ducking into some place of business. In the movies, people are always meeting attractive singles at the dry cleaner, while waiting for their shirts to materialize. In real life, you are more likely to encounter no one except for the elderly proprietor of the establishment, who may not speak sufficient English to grasp your subtle innuendo. No matter. All you have to do is take in a pair of pants to be altered, and before you know it, he'll be on his knees in the back room, groping at your ankles.

What about the gym? The gym is a great place to search for love if you enjoy meeting people who smell vaguely of stationary bicycle seat and are endowed with room temperature IQs. If you don't, the gym is probably just a good place to go to get your reading done. If, however, you managed to get past your rampant intelligencism and learned to appreciate someone for their looks alone, a gym romance might be just the thing. Just remember, when your sweaty new friends say "six-pack" and "get ripped," they are not thinking what you're thinking.

Which leads to the only viable places to meet anybody: bars. Meeting people in bars is simple, mess-free, and it works! Simply select an establishment and begin ordering drinks until the love of your life walks in the door. Don't worry if it takes longer than you expect. Just repeat the pattern until all your friends and relatives come over to your house one day and regale you with colorful anecdotes that don't ring a bell. Then simply select an AA meeting and wait patiently until the love of your life walks in the door.

How to Flirt

Conversational patterns established in the final stages of relationship meltdown do not translate easily into first-date banter. Some important rules of thumb for communicating with a first date after the protracted demise of a long-term relationship:

- Never begin a statement with "you always" or "you never," as it is still too soon to tell which way things will go.
- It is considered impolite to glare.
- Discussing a relationship before it exists can result in awkward silences.

In the old days, flirting involved extensive eye contact and elaborate hand and lip gestures (including flourishes, restrained half-smiles, and the fluttering of fingers about the nose and face). Naturally, a great deal of importance was placed on it, as getting wasted and laid at a frat/office/Christmas party or wedding was pretty much out of the question until about halfway through the twentieth century. Dropping a glove was a good way to initiate a conversation—assuming, of course, that someone was on hand to retrieve it. Sadly, these gestures had a tendency to go unnoticed or to be mistaken for things they were not, such as nose picking and the waving away of flies.

Today, we don't have the time or the patience. Subtle gestures are no longer appreciated in our fast-paced society, and it takes far more aggressive tactics to get noticed. If the behavior of movie, TV, and video game heroines is anything to go by, female attractiveness has little to do with eyelash fluttering and plenty to do with running strenuously, wielding a gun, and brandishing an insult. Because of this, it sometimes can be hard to tell if someone is flirting with you or merely being hostile.

Don't worry if you can't tell the difference.* Radical changes in social and political mores have led to a significant transformation in the age-old art of flirting, leaving many confused as to how to go about doing it. What might have been considered charmingly saucy in another era could easily result in an unpleasant lawsuit today. For this and other reasons having to do with women's studies curricula, MTV's programming schedule, and the enduring popularity of alcohol, flirting today falls largely into three categories: defensive, offensive, and drunk. It should be pointed out, however, that flirting has always contained subtle elements of aggression, as a cursory glance at any good dictionary will reveal.

Flirting: An Etymological Time Line

1553—To toss or casually throw something away, to throw or propel with a jerk or sudden movement, or fillip.

---

* By the same token, don't be surprised if someone thinks you are flirting with them, when you are merely being hostile. One time, I yelled at the cable guy for a solid half hour when he tried to charge me for plugging the cable into my TV in order to improve the reception. When I was quite finished, he asked me out. "You seem very strong. I like that in a woman," he said.

Also, to rap or fillip, to give quick or sudden motion to, to flick.

Mid-1600s—To turn up one's nose, to sneer, gibe, scoff.

Late 1600s—To move with a jerk, or spring, to spring, dart.

1777—To play at courtship, to practice coquetry. Often with a person.

1859—To play or trifle with something.

Modern day—To play or trifle with someone.

Aspiring flirts are often counseled to make prolonged eye contact with the object of their desire. Prolonged lip contact also works. If all goes well, prolonged genital contact will follow.

Let's Explore This Vibe

Janice and Roberta are roommates, both newly single. Though they have bonded over their respective breakups, they have since grown apart. Roberta has taken to brooding, while Janice has systematically begun to throw herself into things in which she claims to have always had an interest. The more Janice plays the bongos, makes mosaics out of shattered hand-mirrors, and tries to get Roberta to sign up for gospel aerobics, the more it plucks Roberta's nerves. "I need a boyfriend," Roberta snaps. "I'm not the kind of girl who does *activities*." Though the same could have once been said for Janice, she says, "I've really matured since last month."

Tensions are unusually high because Janice and Roberta have simultaneously developed an interest in a neighbor they had tacitly agreed was to be nothing more than a "friend." When Max, Janice, and Roberta go out to a party together, Max seems to flirt with both of them equally. Janice savors the feeling of intrigue and vague possibility that comes with being single. What if, she wonders, he winds up falling in love? What if certain feelings inevitably blossom? Janice wonders how Roberta will take it.

As they enter their building together late one night, Roberta suddenly grabs Max by the arm and whispers, "Let's explore this vibe," in his ear, loud enough for Janice to hear. Max and Roberta disappear into Roberta's room laughing, leaving Janice to lie awake half the night, feeling like a real asshole.

What to Expect When Expecting a Call

The telephone is the cornerstone of modern relationships. Without the phone, far fewer dates would be made. Also, far fewer dates would be broken, as people find it difficult to say unpleasant things to one another's faces.

Is he really going to call? It's the first question the hopeful person waiting for a phone call asks herself, yet it's unfortunately not a question that is easily answered. While you may experience some unfamiliar changes as the question gestates in the mind, these do not guarantee that the call is forthcoming. Though symptoms can begin as early as the day the call is promised, they may be a sign that something else is wrong.

Signs That You're Expecting a Phone Call

When	Signs/Symptoms	Other Possible Causes of Discomfort
Morning of Day of Appointed Call	Euphoria, slight dizziness, shortness of breath, and diminished appetite. Lively imagined conversation going splendidly in head.	Dehydration, noctambulism
Afternoon of Day of Appointed Call	Ongoing imaginary conversation continues to elicit raucous laughter. Possible scaring of self	Denial, jet lag

When	Signs/Symptoms	Other Possible Causes of Discomfort
	followed by a stern self-talking to.	
Evening of Day of Appointed Call	Euphoria mellows into pleasant warm glow. Warm glow occasionally spiked with pangs of doubt. Pangs of doubt quickly quashed with bursts of optimism and idea for good joke to use in upcoming call.	Hormonal imbalance, bipolar disorder
Later in Evening of Day of Appointed Call	Mental conversation remains amusing yet becomes slightly less pronouncedly so. Some self-congratulation on impressive display of restraint as evidenced by turning down volume on delusional witty repartee (which was perhaps too frivolous and slightly hysterical anyway) and not picking up the phone and calling.	Seasonal allergies, logomania
Later Still in Evening of Day of Appointed Call	Phone glaring, frequent urination	Vertigo, cystitis
Midnight	Pleasant feeling of melancholy subsides into feeling of mawkish longing.	Inebriation, hypoglycemia, beriberi
1:00 A.M.	Sudden, lively interest in ceiling patterns	Insomnia, despair

When	Signs/Symptoms	Other Possible Causes of Discomfort
Day Two	Tingling, tender, swollen eyeballs, persistent hope	Thyroid problem, depressive psychosis
Day Three	Existential nausea, swollen resentment, darkening under eyes	Existential hangover, gout
Two Weeks On	Intermittently painful memories, food cravings, crying jags	Ebola virus

I Want to Grow Old with You

Martin has been making desultory passes at Samantha for going on a decade now. She's been halfheartedly turning him down for just as long. Samantha has always liked hanging out with Martin, so she wonders if maybe she should give it a shot after all this time. The funny thing is, now that she and her boyfriend have broken up, Martin has decided that he needs a little more time before getting involved. This is okay with Samantha, except that since they sleep together once in a while, it seems strange not to hang out more often. Martin says that he just wants to take it slowly so as not to "ruin it." Samantha knows he's right, but she's starting to hate him a little. When she tells him so, he says, "Okay, I mean, I don't want to completely give up on the possibility, so if it's now or never, let's just go out now." This usually takes the wind out of Samantha's sails, and she agrees to take it slowly. When she gets off the phone, though, she hates him a little more for some reason.

The Tragic Decline
of the Epistolary Romance

Before the invention of the telephone, people who were in love but not in the same room were forced to communicate by letter. Generally speaking, this was tedious and time-consuming. Also, it was sometimes hard to think of what to say.

And there were other problems. Errant letters could easily wind up in the hands of unscrupulous charwomen and rapacious blackguards who would think nothing of blackmailing an unsuspecting swain or his frail paramour. This could result in bankruptcy, public scandals, duels, legally enforceable expectations of marriage, and premature death. Naturally, because of the risks inherent in putting amorous feelings in writing, people thought long and hard before allowing their inflamed passions to lead them to plume and parchment.

Impressive as old, famous love letters may seem at first glance, careful analysis reveals that the sentiments expressed in these were not much different from the sentiments contained in your average modern love phone call. Consider:

Letter #1
To: Nora Barnacle
From: James Joyce
It has just struck me. I came in at half past eleven. Since then I have been sitting in an easy chair like a fool. I could do nothing. I hear nothing but your voice. I am like a fool hear-

ing you call me "Dear." I offended two men today by leaving them coolly. I wanted to hear your voice, not theirs. When I am with you I leave aside my contemptuous, suspicious nature. I wish I felt your head on my shoulder. I think I will go to bed. I have been a half-hour writing this thing. Will you write something to me? I hope you will. How am I to sign myself? I won't sign anything at all, because I don't know what to sign myself.

Translation:
You there? What are you doin'? What are you doin' now? How about now? Now? Call me later. It's me.

Letter #2
To: Felice Bauer
From: Franz Kafka
Write to me only once a week, so that your letter arrives on Sunday—for I cannot endure your daily letters, I am incapable of enduring them. For instance, I answer one of your letters, then lie in bed in apparent calm, but my heart beats through my entire body and is conscious only of you. I belong to you; there is really no other way of expressing it, and that is not strong enough. But for this very reason I don't want to know what you are wearing; it confuses me so much that I cannot deal with life; and that's why I don't want to know that you are fond of me. If I did, how could I, fool that I am, go on sitting in my office, or here at home, instead of leaping onto a train with my eyes shut and opening them only when I am with you? Oh, there is a sad, sad reason for not doing so. To make it short: My health is only just good enough for myself alone, not good enough for marriage, let alone fatherhood. Yet when I read your letter, I feel I could overlook even what cannot possibly be overlooked.

Translation:
I think we should spend a little less time together. It's not you, it's me. If it wasn't me, I wouldn't be leaving this on your machine. I'm a big jerk. You deserve better.

Letter #3
To: Professor Constantin Héger
From: Charlotte Brontë
Monsieur, the poor have not need of much to sustain them—they ask only for the crumbs that fall from the rich man's table. But if they are refused the crumbs they die of hunger. Nor do I, either, need much affection from those I love. I should not know what to do with a friendship entire and complete—I am not used to it. But you showed me of yore a little interest, when I was your pupil in Brussels, and I hold on to the maintenance of that little interest—I hold on to it as I would hold on to life. (Letter was not returned.)

Translation:
Hi. Call me when you get this. I left you a message earlier. Maybe you didn't get it. Did you get my e-mail? I tried to IM you, but I guess you weren't at your desk. That was me, "CharBro"! Okay, um, well. Call me. Bye. Okay. Bye. Maybe I'll try your cell.

The Triumphant Return
of the Epistolary Romance

While it's true that technological advances introduced in the last decade have made it possible for men and women to fail to communicate in sundry new ways, they have also made it easier for people to think long and hard about what to say and how to say it before blurting out "I love you," or some other thing that they will live to regret.

Before e-mail, people relied on clumsy and ineffectual verbal editing methods to present an idealized image of themselves to others. Phrases such as "Scratch that," "Forget it," and "The jury will disregard that last statement" were never very effective in undoing the damage caused by impulsive declarations of love or insecurity.

Furthermore, e-mail allowed garden-variety obsessive types to bypass the embarrassment of picking up and putting down a phone every five seconds, and focus instead on crafting the perfect e-mail response—an activity that can easily fill ten long, nail-biting hours. And it's so much more subtle! Consider the discreet, friendly "Ping!" of an e-mail message landing in your box. Now compare this to the hysterical clang of a ringing phone. How would you rather introduce yourself?

Gracious and subtle a form of harassment as e-mailing is, it can also lead to unattractive obsessive-compulsive behaviors. Every day, you will plant little electronic seeds and kill yourself softly waiting for them to sprout. Try to avoid spending hours a day glued to the monitor slapping at the keyboard like a trained rat in search of a pellet. If you find you cannot control yourself, at least be thankful that nobody is around to witness your behavior. Also, try to avoid overly long and clever responses, which will only make you seem dull-witted in person. Nothing will betray your overexcited feelings more than a "casual" thousand-word reply to a casual greeting.

Singlehood FAQs

Q: What is being single?

A: Being single means being alone for extended periods of time. Whether "long" is a day or a year depends on your personal tolerance for introspection. When you are single, you will be forced, on occasion, to face reality for once. If this causes you instantly to crumble into a million pieces and begin that long series of desperate calls to friends and family, begging them to take responsibility for your life, you may want to reconsider taking that time for yourself. Why not wrap it in a lovely package and hand it to—that guy over there?

Q: Why do I feel so very, very alone?

A: Chances are very few people will take you up on your offer. Eventually, they will stop returning your calls. It would take a village to deal with your insecurities, and you don't live in a village. An apartment building could, in theory, perform the same function, but you find your neighbors are reluctant to water your plants when you go away for the weekend, let alone tend to your multifarious emotional needs.

Q: Why am I so pathetic when I'm single?

A: This is a question that is best discussed with your therapist. If you don't have a therapist, find one immediately. Your new therapist should ideally be young, inexperienced, and

sexually attracted to you. When you tell him about your ex-
boyfriend, or the guy who's currently messing with your
head, he will become explosively angry and may even get
turned on. This will make you feel better.

Q: Is anyone good at being single?
A: Some people are good at being single. These also tend to
be fit, well-organized, financially secure people who abbre-
viate muscle names and say things like "utilize" and "at this
point in time." You probably don't even know many of them,
and they're not too interested in knowing you, either.

Q: What kinds of things can I do for fun when I'm single?
A: Most single people enjoy spending their time trolling for
love, blaming their parents, or weeping into their cats' fur.
Other activities include snorkeling, crochet, and suicidal
ideation.

Q: How can I find a boyfriend?
A: Keep making those desperate calls to friends. Eventually,
somebody will return your call. This person is known as
your "brand-new boyfriend."

Q: How can I find a boyfriend if that doesn't work?
A: The truth is, potential boyfriends are everywhere. You
just have to keep your eyes peeled and your expectations low.
It's important to believe in the abundance of mediocre
potential boyfriends in the world. If you find that your standards are unrealistically high, just think of your last boyfriend. What was so special about him? Wasn't it clear from
the beginning that it was never going to work? It was to all
your friends, since you kept telling them all the gruesome
details.

Q: How can I make sure this never, ever happens to me again?

A: The next time you find yourself sulking across the apartment while your boyfriend watches yet another *NYPD Blue* marathon, just remember, it could be worse. You could be turning all that anger against yourself.

PART FOUR

And So It Begins . . . Again

Behold the Wrong Boyfriend

Maybe you are wondering, "What if I have committed to the serial monogamist lifestyle, and suddenly, out of nowhere, I happen upon my soul mate? What should I do? How can I ensure that I don't start a relationship I can't finish?"

This is an excellent question. Nothing is more embarrassing to a serial monogamist than finding true love. The best way to avoid this is by repeatedly falling in love with one of the following types:*

The Mingler

Charming, funny, and impressively skilled at working a room, the Mingler is a snappy dresser with a mouth that more than makes up for that nose/bald patch/walleye/gout. While you never thought you could feel sexually attracted to a guy like the Mingler, his puckish charm will grow on you. You find yourself gradually warming to the idea until you thaw completely and leave an embarrassing puddle on the

* In doing so it is advisable to select the type that least resembles your previous love, as too many similarities may dampen your initial enthusiasm for the relationship. Your enthusiasm should not begin to moisten until at least three months into the relationship, and preferably until after you have moved in together.

floor, at which point the Mingler will excuse himself and move on.

Mr. Crusty

A proponent of the view that beauty is on the inside, at least when it comes to him, Mr. Crusty always has several projects of a creative nature cooking at once. He doesn't have time to shower, so don't hassle him. In fact, it is possible that Mr. Crusty may not yet own a shower. This is because Mr. Crusty lives in a warehouse, loft, or other formerly industrial, now stealthily toxic "space" with inadequate heating, which he is remodeling himself. This accounts for his interesting coloring, which is actually ground-in soot, and his shortness of cash.

The Trust Fundamentalist

The Trust Fundamentalist is very intense, having had years of leisure to devote to honing his intensity. Like many rich people who have never worked a day in their lives, the Trust Fundamentalist may have a slightly skewed view of the glittery universe that revolves around him. It's not his fault if he is easily distracted. He may ask you to marry him on the first date, a sure sign that he will not ask you out on a second.

Johnny Hurt

Johnny Hurt can trace the roots of his anguish for three generations. Naturally, he is cautious. Though willing to "do the work" from the second date forward, he is, unfortunately, far less willing to "do the fun." While at first you will want to care for and nurture Johnny Hurt, you will soon want to hurt him, too.

Mr. Successful

Are you the other half in the power couple he envisions? Are you beautiful enough to make his friends want to rip their own heads off? Does your father own a media empire? Does your mother own a Brazilian coffee plantation? If you cannot answer yes to any of these questions, you might want to reconsider your interest in Mr. Successful. Mr. Successful does not fool around. That's why he's Mr. Successful.

The Urban Outdoorsman

The Urban Outdoorsman loves nothing better than being alone in the woods, which is why he moved to the city. Clearly, the urban outdoorsman has many issues, which will not soon be resolved. Do not be confused if the Urban Outdoorsman expects you to keep up his jaunty pace while you are shod in heels. The Urban Outdoorsman is a great believer in sensible footwear, even when attending well-heeled events at well-paved locales.

Child of the Universe

The Child of the Universe is a great person to meet after life has beaten you down. He will impress you with his willingness to ask the universe for everything and anything he needs. Unfortunately, the universe is usually busy and rarely gets back to him. He will then impress you with his willingness to ask *you* for anything and everything he needs, including the rent money.

The Aspiring Genius

The Aspiring Genius has certain priorities, none of which include you. Highly sensitive and emotional when it comes to his art, his greatest and most lasting passion will always be reserved for his critics, especially when they act as though he doesn't exist. If you are interested in an Aspiring Genius, you would do well to follow this example. If your lack of interest fails to arouse his, try giving him a nasty review. This will never fail to elicit a passionate response.

The Drummer

Any person who enjoys hitting pot-shaped things with sticks has not managed to make the transition from the anal to the oral stage.

Singing in the Rain Check

Sarah and James met, quite by accident, and within days James was calling Sarah three times a day. He sometimes embarrassed her by putting his nose inside her navel while she stood around in somebody's kitchen trying to make a complicated point. In the second week of their relationship, Sarah went out of town and James insisted on picking her up at the airport when she returned. When she arrived, he wasn't there. She waited around for a while and then called. He was really sorry, he said. Sarah got angry, and James explained that he wasn't really ready for a girlfriend. Three years later they are still together. Sometimes, Sarah still wonders what he meant by "girlfriend."

Things to Do on a Date–
If, In Fact, That's What This Is

What does "dating" really mean nowadays? Must a plan be involved? Is food required? Does fooling around with an out-of-town stranger at a party count? What about sitting around at a bar getting drunk and exercised about cultural imperialism? Can you date someone more than once before he officially becomes your boyfriend? Does an MTV crew need to be present?

Some of the confusion surrounding "dates" arises from the fact that people, as a people, are reluctant to ask for what they want for fear of getting it and then deciding they want something else. People say things they don't mean and keep their true feelings hidden—usually someplace where they can't find them when they really need them and are already running late.

Not asking for a date is far cooler than asking for one directly, and it is also an acceptable way to avoid responsibility for initiating a romance and provides a useful loophole for getting out of it later. Rather than saying, "Let's go out on a date," and sounding hopelessly earnest and creepy, most people choose to go with something like "We should get our dogs together."

Naturally, this leads to some confusion. Thinking that you have been asked out on a "date" when you have merely been asked to keep someone company while they eat can result in mortifying misunderstandings and costly check-splitting scenarios. And yet, as we have just seen, many an enduring love affair has begun with the immortal words "I'm not really looking for a girlfriend right now."

Today, most people who go out on actual dates do so on TV. Many people would rather rely on seasoned professionals than on their friends to set them up with someone nice. That way, when the date turns out to be a borderline retarded frat boy with a slight porn, alcohol, and cash problem, they can blame the seasoned professionals. Others would simply rather spare themselves the trouble of calling up all their friends to tell them about the date later, since their friends will have, naturally, tuned in to watch and jeer. Unfortunately, TV dating has spoiled dating for untelevised couples, who have come to equate "going on a date" with snapping on three inches of fuchsia Spandex, mounting their date on a bar stool, and then mercilessly trashing them in a postdate interview in order to advance their own, nonexistent acting careers.

Whatever you do, don't feel bad about not having been asked out on many dates in your life. "Dating," as such, no longer really exists.* If all goes not so well, it is just a euphemism for how many times you can hang out with someone before engaging in "the talk." If all goes well, the date should flow smoothly into the next decade.

The Date-Date

Traditionally, the date-date is a recreational get-together consisting of dinner, drinks, and sex with no strings attached.

---

* The exception to this is online dating, simply because it requires couples to agree on a mutually convenient time and place for their first meeting. Once the initial meeting has taken place, the couple may revert to more familiar forms of behavior.

Participants are usually two attractive, well-adjusted individuals who realize immediately that they will not be developing feelings for each other. If the feeling is mutual, the date can proceed agreeably apace, never to be repeated again.

The Interview Date

For a date to qualify as an interview date, it must involve at least one professional dater. A professional dater is a person, usually female, with a set of very strict rules gleaned from man-catching manuals and *Fortune* magazine that she follows to the letter.* Should her date fail to follow one of the 2,365 unspoken rules of courtship she has compiled from dating guides ghost-written by an international consortium of proto-fascist grandmothers, the date will not take place. If, on the other hand, he successfully completes the first set of hurdles—sending out an engraved invitation two to three weeks beforehand, for instance—the professional dater may deign to grace his chartered hot-air balloon with her presence. Once comfortably seated at table, she will proceed to barrage him with a series of questions designed to determine compatibility, sperm count, and net worth. If he finds this line of questioning enjoyable, they should be very happy together.

The Love Date, Unrequited

The unrequited love date also begins as a simple date-date. However, for one of the parties involved, it does not end for

---

* Men can also be professional daters. The male professional dater is a person with a very strict set of physical requirements, usually gleaned from *Hustler.*

anywhere from a week to three months afterward. Misinterpreting your date's attempt to charm the pants off you as something deeper and more meaningful than an attempt to charm the pants off you, you may embark on a long period of focused analysis and introspection, dissecting the date for clues as to why no other dates have been forthcoming.

One way to tell that the object of your affection has no intention of flinging himself headlong into a relationship is if you never get any of his valuable social real estate. If your torrid lovemaking sessions are usually preceded by a Sunday brunch, a Tuesday night jaunt to the supermarket, or a quiet Thursday afternoon spent waiting for the UPS guy, you can be sure that you are now firmly ensconced in a temporal ghetto from which you will not readily escape.

For unrequited love dating to occur, it's not necessary to have a date in the first place. In fact, lengthy one-sided alliances can also spring from casual conversations conducted over the bean-dip bowl at a friend's Super Bowl party, even if the bean dip was itself the subject of conversation. Casual remarks such as "See you later" or "There's something on your chin" can be easily misconstrued by the overly amorous as signs of interest. Does "See you later" mean simply "Good-bye"? Or could it mean "I'll *definitely* be seeing *you* later, as soon as I coyly procure your number from our delightful host"? By the same token, could "There's something on your chin" be code for "I'm afraid of the depth of emotion I might experience should I let myself become close to someone as intoxicating and unforgettable as you"? It's up to you to decide.

Once you have homed in on the object of your interest— whether it be at a local Starbucks or simply in passing on the street—it is important to imbue that person with every quality you wish for in a mate. The fact that he is unemployed, for example, will strike you as piquantly liberated and free-spirited. Chillingly aggressive yet impersonal sexual advances will come off as adorably childlike and impulsive. His postcoital decision to drive you home at four in the morning, rather than face waking up with you the next day, will take on a gallant patina, which will only add to your favorable impression of his commitment to getting to work on time the next day.

The Love Date, Requited

Do you believe in love at first sight? No? How about co-dependence? While the former may still be rare, the latter is far more common than most people realize. The requited love date rarely begins as a planned activity, as people who fall instantly in love usually lack the foresight to actually plan things. An ideal date of this kind might involve two lovelorn serial monogamists getting together over several pints to share their sense of bitterness, hopelessness, and loss. If all goes reasonably well, both parties will conclude at the end of it that love has at long last been found.*

The Wedding Date

Hasty marriages have enjoyed a revival in recent years, largely thanks to the fact that the children of the seventies and eighties are rebelling against their lecherous divorced parents and the fact that their dads' new wives are usually younger than they are. The urge to legally merge has taken on tsunami-like proportions, spawning untold narratives about chic urban girls with nice shoes desperately trying to

* See Part Six, "The Five-Year Breakup Plan."

land a husband by the recently extended sell-by date of thirty-five. This marital tidal wave has also spawned an epidemic of junior divorces. In fact, today's young marriages often seem to last about as long as it takes to return the silver to the caterer. And many young broken families are surmising what most serial monogamists have known all along—that divorce is just like breaking up, only with paperwork.

What Sex Means

While sex is an excellent way to burn excess calories and get one's mind off the phone bill, it should never be confused with something it is not.

Many people view sex as an unspoken, unwritten contract between two people who, having spent some time on top of each other, should then proceed to spend the rest of their lives—or at the very least, the rest of the following day—together. This is where many people get into big trouble. While sex is indeed an agreement of sorts, it is no longer considered binding.

In order to avoid confusion, resentment, obsession, depression, agitation, and repeated phone messages, couples planning on sleeping together before learning each other's hobbies, childhood pets' names, and last names might consider entering into a mutually convenient agreement of expectations, a sample of which is outlined herewith:

Sample Precoital Agreement

THIS AGREEMENT, made this _____ day of _____, 20 ____, is between _____ and _____.

PURPOSE. The parties expect to engage in sex in the near future. Each has separate notions, ideas, and expectations regarding what this "means," the nature and extent of which are fully disclosed in the statement of liabilities (Exhibit A of this document). The parties are setting forth in this Agreement their respective rights regarding their sexual involvement and its aftermath. They are also setting forth their rights regarding future sexual interactions, including, but not limited to, kissing, petting, meaningful glances, and follow-up telephone calls.

EFFECT OF AGREEMENT. This Agreement shall take effect only upon the solemnization of sexual intercourse between the parties. Thereafter, each of the parties shall separately retain all rights to feelings, intentions, and expectations resulting from intercourse, as well as unexpected changes of heart experienced separately in the future ("Feelings, Intentions, and Expectations"), and each of them shall have the unrestricted right to act on said Feelings, Intentions, and Expectations, free and clear of any claim that may be made by the other by reason of their sexual involvement and with the same effect as if no sexual involvement had been consummated between them. Feelings, Intentions, and Expectations shall include aforementioned changes of heart, as well as any feelings of attachment, longing, regret, infatuation, and any and all emotions resulting therefrom, as well as from any secondary emotions derived from such feelings.

FEELINGS, INTENTIONS, AND EXPECTATIONS. The parties agree that the feelings and expectations created by this Agreement have emotional value to each of the parties and each of the parties agrees to make no claim to the Emotions of the other party, either during the joint lives of the parties hereto or thereafter, and to indemnify the other party against all feelings of guilt, torment, or responsibility arising from any such claim.

WAIVER OF RIGHTS. Except as otherwise provided in this Agreement, each party hereby waives, releases, and relinquishes any and all right or interest whatsoever in the other's immediate or future thoughts, feelings, or social prospects, including but not limited to weekend, holiday, and vacation plans.

DISSOLUTION/SEPARATION/ANNULMENT. Except as otherwise provided in this Agreement, each party specifically agrees that neither shall make any claim for or be entitled to receive any continuing affection, regard, or devotion, including, but not limited to, any claims for services rendered, dinners purchased, and labor expended by either of the parties during any period prior to the sexual encounter.

COHABITATION. Each party waives any and all rights or claims existing now or hereafter existing to bring up the subject of cohabitation.

RIGHT TO CONTEST. Neither party shall maintain any claim or demand whatsoever against the other for intimacy, affection, attachment, partiality, or exclusive attraction, which is either inconsistent with or not provided for in this Agreement.

ACKNOWLEDGMENTS. Each party acknowledges that he or she has had an adequate opportunity to read and study this Agreement, to consider it, to consult with attorneys individually selected by each party, without any form of coercion, duress, or pressure. Each party acknowledges that he or she has examined the Agreement before signing it, and has been advised by independent legal counsel concerning the rights, liabilities, and implications of this document.

STATE LAW. It is intended that this Agreement be valid
and enforceable within the provisions of (Statute #) of the
State Law, and that Case Law which governs its interpretation.

PART FIVE

Monogamy, Serial Thriller

Do You Love Me,
or Am I Just Paranoid?

You are considering embarking on a new romantic adventure, or you have already taken a few wobbly steps in that direction, when suddenly you are seized by fear. Fear is a natural, self-preserving instinct, useful in helping people escape from marauding bears. But, at times, fear can seem irrational, unwarranted, the product of an overripe imagination. Are you justifiably cautious, or are you just paranoid?

The *Mayo Clinic Family Health Book* defines paranoid personality disorder as a condition that causes a formerly sane person to become suspicious and overly sensitive to perceived injuries, slights, and tricks by others. It can also be defined as a psychotic condition marked by well-systematized, logically consistent delusions. Both definitions also inadvertently describe the love condition, which is cause for concern.

Is fear of love equal to a state of mental derangement? Or is it a normal, instinctive response to perceived danger?

Let's investigate. When a person is attacked by a marauding bear, she rarely experiences self-doubt. She does not ask herself if she should give the marauding bear a chance to get to know her better. Chased by a marauding bear, she will not think to herself, "Maybe this bear is different from other marauding bears." She will not wonder if the bear's interest is sincere or whether she is unfairly lumping all marauding bears into one category. She will not mistake the bear's advances for signs of love, or worry that the bear may be insincere in his affections. As a person runs from a marauding bear, she will rarely pause to wonder if her flight is justified or if the problem is simply in her head.

Fear of bears, however, is an occasional fear unrelated to other fears. Conversely, fear of love is chronic, comprehensive, and cumulative. When a person fears a marauding bear, he does not take into consideration past experiences with other bears, friends' and parents' experiences with bears, or examples of bear-man connections in literature.

Fear of love tends to curdle over time, forming an emotional bolus that obstructs instinct and leads to highly sophisticated and evasive modes of thought. When a person is attacked by a marauding bear, questions of motivation, sincerity, and intent rarely enter the picture. It is the rare person who asks himself if the bear intends to stick around after it is finished marauding. It is the rarer person still who wonders whether a bear is just messing with her head and really has no intention of marauding at all.

In the grip of love paranoia, a person will also subject her own mental health to intense self-scrutiny. Love paranoia is a doubting fear; a fear that doesn't even trust itself. Attacked by a marauding bear, most people do not wonder whether they are insane for even entertaining the possibility of a meaningful relationship with the bear. They do not worry that, by automatically running away from the bear, they might be robbing themselves of one of life's richest experiences. They are confident in their decision to flee the bear, as clearly the bear's intention is to maraud.

Of course, the bear-love comparison only takes us so far. Bears are unlikely to try to lure victims with promises of exotic voyages abroad or baskets of fancy fruit. Straightforward by nature, bears make no promises they cannot keep and are unlikely to attempt to disguise their intent to maraud as anything other than what it is. Therefore, there is considerably less opportunity for confusion when one is being attacked by a marauding bear than there is when one is being pursued by a potential mate.

Finally, failure to outrun a marauding bear, though painful and potentially fatal, is not generally exacerbated by a vague sense of unease, the sensation that one is being unfairly scrutinized, jealousy, the sinking sensation that one has fallen for a trick, the panicky sensation that one is ensnared in a trap, and the feeling that one would sooner confront a marauding bear than fall in love again.

In Love or Insane?

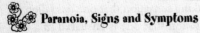 **Paranoia, Signs and Symptoms**

- Abuse of alcohol or other drugs
- Withdrawal from friends and family
- Loss of interest in daily activities
- Inability to concentrate
- Glazed or faraway stare
- Decline in academic, athletic, or job performance
- Inappropriate dressing for weather or occasion

Love, Signs and Symptoms

- Abuse of alcohol or other drugs
- Withdrawal from friends and family
- Loss of interest in daily activities
- Inability to concentrate
- Glazed or faraway stare
- Decline in academic, athletic, or job performance
- Inappropriate dressing for weather or occasion

Paranoia, Perceptions

- Extreme or unusual sensitivity to light/colors/noise
- Believing his or her thoughts are controlled by others
- Fear of being touched by others

♥ Changed sense of self (believing body parts are diseased, detached, hanging, etc.)
♥ Sense of body boundaries deteriorating

Love, Perceptions

♥ Extreme or unusual sensitivity to light/colors/noise
♥ Believing his or her feelings are controlled by others
♥ Fear of not being touched by others
♥ Changed sense of self (believing body parts are fat, stubby, hairy, small)
♥ Sense of emotional boundaries deteriorating

I Love You Like a Son, Whatever Your Name Is

Dave and Hope have been together for three years, and have spent many Christmases together at her family's house in New Jersey. Hope's mom loves Dave. She really does. "He's a darling boy," she says. "And such a talented writer! One day the world will see that. But like he says, some of the greatest talents were ignored until it was too late and they were dead."

The problem is that Hope's mom has a little trouble getting Dave's name right. Before meeting Dave, Hope went out with Michael; before Michael, she lived with John. Before John there was Jake. Hope's mom has a hard enough time keeping her children's names straight, often running through the entire list including both dogs before hitting on the correct nomenclature. Unfortunately, she has no trouble remembering all of Hope's exes' names, in order, before arriving at the present. It would be okay, except that Dave secretly suspects that neither Hope nor Hope's mom is entirely over Jake, John, and Michael, and it makes him a little sulky.

Making Love Work

If popular notions about evolutionary theory are anything to go by, men and women were not put upon this earth to be each other's snookums. Of course, nobody goes by popular notions about evolutionary theory anymore except for not-very-bright guys explaining to their girlfriends why they don't want to be their snookums anymore.

One thing is certain, however: several billion years of evolution, a few thousand years of civilization, and a number of best-selling etiquette manuals have made it possible for the average human to approach another member of the species with intentions other than screwing or killing them.* We can now kill people with kindness or screw them up without ever removing our pants. Yes, sticks and stones may be lethal if handled with sufficient force, but words can inflict deep wounds on a tender psyche. Naturally, you want to protect yourself from the casual cruelties of others. But how can you do so and still remain open to love's rich rewards? How can you tell the difference between a charming aside and an elaborately coded insult? How can you avoid rejection, or at the very least, ensure that it only comes along once every two to five years?

The best way to do this is to commit to a relationship early, before any of the trouble begins. This way, when problems

---

* However, these also remain popular.

invariably arise down the line, you will be locked into an agreement that requires "working on the relationship," or, as it is also known, "quarreling bitterly."

Over and over again, we are told that "relationships are work." Yet few of us are ever paid or promoted. What exactly does "working" on a relationship entail?

A Gung Ho Attitude

First, it is important that you throw yourself into the relationship energetically, ignoring any misgivings you might have. If this is going to work, you're going to have to trust your instincts. If your instincts tell you that the fact that he just quit his corporate law job to become a yoga instructor, welder, and full-time "searcher" will not present a problem down the line, go ahead and trust them. Just keep in mind that instincts are not known for their life-management skills or financial acumen.

A Firm Grasp of the Technology

First, it is necessary for the two of you to locate each other's "buttons" and begin pushing them ceaselessly, though not in an obvious way. This is a relatively easy procedure and one that comes naturally to most couples. One person's "issues" are another's "needs." For example, if "communicating" is one of your needs, then "space" will be one of his "issues." If "jealousy" is one of his issues, then "freedom" will be one of your needs. If everything is functioning properly, you should quickly reach the point where hurting each other becomes as simple as being yourselves.

A Commitment to Commitment

Just like at work, there will be times when you look up at the four flimsy, carpeted walls of your relationship and ask yourself what, exactly, you are doing there. You will wonder if you have wandered into a dead end and stayed there out of fear of venturing out on your own. You will grow concerned about your future prospects and ask yourself why nobody else ever makes the coffee. Then you will remember that, in this economy, you are lucky to have a relationship. Address any nagging misgivings the way members of the business community do, by repeating senseless but reassuring catchphrases to yourself. Tell yourself there's "too much on your plate right now" and that you can't possibly think about striking out on your own until you have "all your ducks in a row" and "all your pigs in a blanket." If doubts persist, tell yourself doubts are a healthy sign that you have not "drunk the Kool-Aid" or "put on the sneaker." Then stay put. Nothing will have changed, but you should experience a pleasant feeling of self-satisfaction.

Managing That Jittery Pre-Layoff Period

This period is also an excellent time to indulge in self-destructive behaviors you may have sworn off. For example, during a big blowout, it is permissible to pour oneself a large glass of Scotch and down it in one dramatic gulp. Go ahead and raid the medicine cabinet for that cough syrup with codeine. Run out and see what an old boyfriend is doing at three A.M. After all, you are in pain, and pain should never go unmedicated.* The old axiom about never going to bed angry is true. You should go to bed feeling sad, hopeless, and emotionally drained.

---

* Except, perhaps, during childbirth, now that it is trendy to allow oneself to "feel" an episiotomy but not a bad mood.

PART SIX

The Five-Year
Breakup Plan

Meeting the Family

Before getting down on your parents for failing to greet your newest boyfriend with an enthusiasm bordering on hysteria, take a moment to consider what it feels like for them. Honestly, they've been through so much already.

Still, if your parents are like most parents, they would sooner sign over the title of the house to your new boyfriend than admit to hating him on sight. As a result, they will claim to love him immediately. Nobody wants to be the heavy.

Your parents may, in fact, be bald-faced liars, but it's also quite possible that they are having a hard time adapting to the constant change. One way to tell is if they often seem uncomfortable using the word "boy" (as in, "my daughter's—friend") in reference to someone who may have less hair than Grandpa. Most parents also feel uncomfortable using words like "partner," "lover," or "significant other" to describe the man who is preventing their daughter from marrying. Also, most parents tend to withhold their feelings, in the hope that your wrong boyfriend will someday blossom into your right husband. Ultimately, however, they are not stupid. They realize that your new boyfriend, such as he is, might be sticking around for a while and joining them at the Thanksgiving table for the next decade. Realize this, and don't expect them to come out and say what they really think. You might take it the wrong way, or worse, tell your boyfriend what they really think of him. Nobody wants to be choking on the stuffing year after year.

Will You Be Staying Long, Honey?

Willard recently brought Flower, his brand-new girlfriend, home to his parents' house for the weekend. Although Willard and Flower had recently moved in together, his parents had never met her before. Willard met Flower while he was still living with Fiona, his college girlfriend. Willard and Fiona had always planned to get married, each as soon as the other changed a few things about their personality. But after ten years of cohabitation and eight of couples therapy, Willard and Fiona's therapist ordered them to give up.

Willard was secretly relieved, as he had had his eye on Flower, who worked at the local video store, for quite some time. He realized, however, that his parents might not be so thrilled. Fiona, after all, was a pediatrician from Philadelphia, and Flower was an artist with ten rings in her left eyebrow. When they arrived at his parents' house, Willard's mom showed Flower to the guest room. Flower, who had never had Willard's advantages, burst out laughing. Willard took his mom aside and explained that, seeing as they were living together, they would prefer to share a bedroom. Willard's mother's reply surprised him. "Why can't you just sneak across the hall in the middle of the night like your brother does?" she wailed, before bursting into tears.

Dad, the Mother of
All Bad Boyfriends

Have you ever wondered why your relationships are as consistently dysfunctional as they are? Do you suspect that forces beyond your control are affecting their outcome? Are you reluctant to take responsibility for your own behavior? Are you 100 percent faultless in all situations? If you answered yes to all these questions, maybe you should consider blaming your dad.

Blaming your dad is not just for children of psychopaths and perverts anymore. With a little creativity and effort, *anyone* can blame their dad for their failed relationships. The main thing is to keep an open mind about your dad's flaws. Be creative. Don't censor your thoughts. An exaggerated sense of acceptance or generosity toward your dad will only result in the responsibility for the collapse of all of your adult relationships falling squarely back on your shoulders. Why not let Dad shoulder some of it? After all, that's what he's there for. He'd want to help. Really he would.

Thousands of people have blamed their dads for everything from violence to crankiness to high blood pressure. As an accountability shield, it's proven to work. But what should you do, you are probably asking, if you've never blamed your dad for your own personal failings before? What if you don't have the foggiest idea what he ever did wrong?

First, take a deep breath and relax. It's not nearly as difficult as it seems. Take a moment to dwell on the areas of your life that could use improvement but are not likely to see it due to genetic or socioeconomic factors beyond your control. Are your calves slightly bowed? Dad. Fingers stubby? Dad again. Did you fail to spend even one childhood summer in a Bahamian resort? You know who. Second, take the time to dredge up some feelings about these failings. If you have none to draw upon, go ahead and make them up.

Next, figure out exactly what kind of dad you had. This should go a long way in explaining what kind of relationships you choose, and why they are doomed to fail.

Absent Dad

If you are reasonably sure you don't have a dad, don't panic! Absent dad tops the list of bad dads at number one! Not having a dad is the perfect excuse for getting angry whenever your boyfriend fails to call or come over at the appointed time, as this will immediately trigger your abandonment issues. Also, absent dads provide the perfect escape hatch for any relationship. You couldn't trust *him,* how can you expect to trust anyone else? How can they expect to trust you? How, for that matter, can you trust yourself?

Doting Dad

Was yours the kind of dad who drove you to every soccer practice, took you out for ice cream, and listened to your problems? Bastard! There is nothing like the moony devotion of a father figure (particularly if the father figure is actually your father) to set you up on the shaky emotional scaffolding of high expectations. All your life, you have been told that you are special and different—which, as you should have realized by now, are common euphemisms for "re-tarded" and "weird."

Dad Who Can Beat Up Your Dad

Was your dad the silent but violent type? Having grown up a maiden sequestered in an impregnable fortress, you may have developed a saucy sense of adventure. So you like to talk back to muggers and taunt roving groups of drunken frat boys. It's not unreasonable to expect some protection in these circumstances. Your dad could scare anyone away. How were you supposed to know your boyfriend couldn't take on a couple of fat bikers?

Sugar Dad

He wanted to give you the best of everything, and he did: a princess bedroom, your very own pony, and the best "father issues" money can buy. Is it your fault that nothing can satisfy you now? It's not. Right, Daddy?

Your Little Friend

Julie and Stew dated for almost a year, and while Julie had met Stew's entire family, Stew had never met Julie's father, Tom. He had, however, heard enough about him to be very afraid.

Every time Tom would walk up, Stew would dodge out the door or duck around the nearest corner. Tom would say to Julie, "Why's your little friend running away from me? Is he scared or something?" Tom referred to all of Julie's boyfriends as "your little friend." Occasionally, he would refer to Stew as "Mr. Pid," which was the name of a character in a sketch he participated in when his company sent him to anger management camp. Tom thought this very clever. "Get it?" he would say to Julie. "Stew Pid!" Julie would respond in the affirmative. After all, she did get it.

Eventually, Stew and Julie broke up, so Stew never had to meet Tom.

Living Together: The Noncommittal Commitment

Living together provides a more affordable alternative to living alone. It is also a great way to ensure that nuptials will almost certainly never take place. This has little to do with the oft-repeated saw about people who decline to purchase livestock when their dairy products are obtainable gratis. Whether you own your cow or lease it, you are bound to develop a lactose intolerance sooner or later.

When making the decision to move in together, most couples find that one of them doesn't want to. Let's say, for the sake of argument, that the domestically inclined half of that couple is you. And curiously, your partner's reluctance does not stop you from bringing up the subject three times a week over dinner. Why the doomed tenacity? Monogamists are long-term investors by nature. If they manage to hold on long enough, they reason, the reluctant party will eventually get evicted or lose his job, obviating the separate dwelling issue.

After a few months of this, you may begin to develop a deep-seated resentment toward your domestically disinclined partner. And yet it does not occur to you that it may not be such a great idea, happiness-wise, to move in with someone who has been systematically badgered into moving in with you. In fact, your actions are not unlike those of an unsaddled rider clinging tenaciously to the underbelly of a galloping horse. In this situation, most mental health professionals and riding instructors would instruct their clients to simply *let go* lest they be trampled underfoot. You, on the other hand, will continue to hang on for dear life, operating under the misapprehension that if only you can hoist yourself back up to where you were a minute ago, everything will be fine. Obviously, you've never been on a horse.

Let's take a different situation. Say your partner is keen on entering into a domestic arrangement with you as long as this does not require a ceremony to kick it off. Some think of living together as a trial period, much like a test drive. If two people can withstand the daily ups and downs of cohabitation, the conventional wisdom goes, they should go ahead and tie the knot. What most people tend to ignore is that a test drive, which usually lasts no more than half an hour, is designed to give a person just enough of a taste of what it would be like to form a permanent bond with a vehicle as to prompt them to make an impulsive decision that will continue to cost them for years.

Finally, the big day arrives—you and Junior are moving in together! Several days of unpacking boxes and take-out and fun indoor camping follow. You're carrying on like Rock Hudson and Doris Day, when suddenly your partner becomes morally repugnant to you because of the way he lives his life. In these days when morals are all but forgotten, living with someone is a great way to revive these feelings. Simple domestic acts are transformed into ideological battlegrounds, where you, former indifferent slacker, emerge as proud avenger of all that is right, true, and tasteful. Even more distressing, you find that certain elements that had all but disappeared from your life—nagging, phone-hogging, other people's disgusting messes, other people finding your messes disgusting—come back with a vengeance. What many couples forget is that several of the years spent between living with their parents and living with their significant others have most likely been spent living alone. Suddenly, moving in together doesn't look so much like the next step into adulthood as it does like homebound regression.

Some Issues You'll Deal with in Cohabitation

- *Decorating Issues:* Why are your belongings uniformly splendid, while other people's suck? This remains a mystery. What is known is that the best way to deal with such "fun" "personal" items as tattered recliners, uprooted London phone booths, and art made by demented relatives is to deride them mercilessly and without rest.

- *Division of Labor Issues:* The best time to pick up your clothes, do your dishes, or go to the grocery store is when you feel like it. The best time for your partner to do the same is when his mess starts to get on your nerves. Unfortunately, he may feel that the best time for *you* to do these things is when *he* wants you to, which may lead to an impasse. Also, yelling.

- *Privacy Issues:* Too numerous to mention here. Let it be said, however, that the issue of privacy works both ways. Just as all your annoying ticks, habits, and quirks will now be on display twenty-four hours a day, so will you be privy to a panoply of behaviors you never intended to witness.

- *Money Issues:* Now that sex has lost its taboo, the sharing of money can be considered to be the final frontier of intimacy. Most cohabitating couples find that they don't know each other well enough yet.

- *Issues Issues:* As familiarity breeds contempt, so issues breed issues. Before you know it, you will be spending all of your free time engaging in discussions about how you engage in discussions, leaving no time for actual discussions.

As you grapple with this fresh horror, you will likely be bombarded with questions from relatives, friends, coworkers, and telemarketers regarding your civil status and its likelihood to change. Rather than help, these questions often lead to nagging doubts about whether moving in together was such a good idea in the first place. You may eventually conclude that it was nothing more than a de facto breakup, minus the loneliness and expense of maintaining a single household, plus the infrequent sex, silent meals, and sinking feeling that you will ultimately wind up alone anyway. In short, living together provides many of the same opportunities for regret and resentment as marriage, with fewer obligations.

Living Together vs. Marriage: A Handy Guide to Telling Them Apart

Important Decisions

Once a couple has made the important decision to marry, other important decisions seem fun, easy, and relatively inconsequential by comparison. Married couples soon find themselves fervently embracing the entire decision-making process. Questions will naturally form like tiny bubbles: "What should we have for dinner?" "Should we buy a house?" "Should we have a baby?" And "Should we get a divorce?" Conversely, when a cohabiting couple puts off the important decision to marry indefinitely, other important decisions also go by the wayside or are made alone. Cohabiting couples are far more likely than married couples to eschew the conjugal "we" and speak in terse declarative sentences. For example: "I have plans tonight," "I'm pregnant," and "I'm leaving."

Wedding Photos

Most married couples take dozens of photos on their special day. These photos are then prominently displayed all over the couple's house, where they serve as reminders of expensive and stressful nuptials. The photos usually ensure that the couple will think long and hard before ending a relationship and opening the door to the possibility of a second wedding. Conversely, cohabiting couples, who are not aided by such useful reminders, sometimes find themselves staring at bare walls wondering who they are, what they are doing there, and to whom those socks belong.

Family Obligations

Married people are obliged to attend family brunches hosted by their in-laws, laugh at offensive jokes, and make big, good-natured plays for the check. Live-in boyfriends are not obliged to attend the same, not obliged to provide valid excuses for bailing on such functions, and not obliged to feel bad about it. They are, however, obligated to discuss their partner's feelings of betrayal and resentment for far longer than it would have taken to polish off a free plate of eggs Benedict in contemptuous silence. On the other hand, this may be worth it as they will have successfully avoided discussing their "plans" for the "future" with their girlfriend's understandably anxious parents, and then feeling vaguely guilty about letting them pick up the check for the umpteenth time.

Work Parties

Married people are obliged to attend spouse's office Christmas parties, expected to laugh at partner's boss's annoying jokes, and pretend not to notice when boss/boss's wife makes big, drunken play for spouse. Live-in boyfriends are not obliged to attend, not obliged to explain last-minute decision not to attend, and not obliged to feel guilty about the fact that girlfriend's coworkers are starting to suspect they don't exist. On the other hand, this may be worth it, as they will have successfully avoided discussing their "plans" for the "future" with partner's nosy boss.

Friends in Common

Married couples like to ditch old single friends, as they are needless reminders of how pathetic they were when they were single. Rather than be forced to listen to their single or serial monogamist friends lament their single or serial monogamist status, it is much easier and infinitely more pleasant to get together with a new set of matching his and hers married friends to talk about how great things are. Sometimes, this can be most easily accomplished by having a drink in front of the mirror.

Cohabiting couples, on the other hand, tend to hold on to their own friends because they are going to need them. Then they stay home to argue about whose friends to go out with. This can lead to assertions like "My friends are more fun," which can lead to remarks like "Your friends are boring," which can lead to confessions like "My friends hate you, anyway," which can lead to staying home more often.

Literally Inseparable

Brock and Carlotta have been living in the same apartment for going on thirteen years. "It's really kept the relationship together," says Brock. "I don't know where we would be without it." Retorts Carlotta, "Probably living with our parents again." Brock and Carlotta, who reside in New York's trendy East Village, met in college and moved in together when it dawned on them that performance art wasn't going to pay the bills. Says Brock, "We've been together for a long time, and that does something to you. I'm not sure what." Are there wedding bells in the future? "Marriage is a bourgeois construct," Carlotta says, idly fingering a nearby Guatemalan tapestry. Adds Brock, "Yeah, why does our union need to be sanctioned by the state? It's just a piece of paper, right? Plus, we're not really sure we're all that right for each other." Carlotta laughs, then coughs, then adds, "Yeah. We're just taking it one decade at a time."

The Perils of Communication

When two people reach the point where they are no longer able to talk normally, it becomes necessary for them to communicate. Communication is the exclusive province of people who no longer like each other, which is why we rarely communicate with our friends. On the rare occasions that communication between friends does occur, it is generally a sign that one of the friends has become a surrogate boyfriend or girlfriend, and that the two of you are headed for an ugly breakup.

Communication is a form of conversation in which ideas are exchanged like blows in a vain attempt to cudgel the "truth" from another individual. Because the truth is rarely pleasant, to say nothing of amusing, partners intent on communicating should reflect on the possible outcomes of their attempts to extract it from their partners. Often, it involves forcing another person to sit down and listen to all the reasons you hate them, then impugning their emotional development when they balk at having to listen. Most people have not reached the stage of spiritual evolution that allows them to sit down and take this.

For example, most people react badly to the following:

1. We have to talk.
2. He's just someone I used to know.
3. Look, don't take this the wrong way.

4. It's just a work party. You wouldn't have a good time.
5. She's got a boyfriend, okay?
6. Yeah, sure, let's get together. How about Tuesday morning, sevenish?
7. Do you ever think about other people?
8. Everyone thinks you should just chill out.
9. I've done this a million times, okay?
10. The doctor says it's just a rash.

In these times of increased communication between partners, words get thrown around that we cannot or will not back up with action. Today, "Will you marry me?" is considered an appropriate way to express appreciation for a good joke or a nice dinner. Accepting an impromptu proposal is considered bad form and can lead to uncomfortable discussions.

If you have determined that you are equipped to handle whatever comes out of your partner's mouth, you may proceed with your attempts to communicate. However, if you find that your lover is reluctant to listen to you when you unleash your resentments onto him or her, perhaps you should reexamine your approach. Do you tend to focus on yourself and your needs exclusively? When it comes to communicating with your partner, are you selfish or selfless?

Selfish Subjects for Discussion

♥ My feelings
♥ My feelings about you
♥ My feelings about your reaction to my feelings about you

To better get your point across, consider the other person's feelings and point of view. Instead of focusing on yourself, try concentrating on your partner. Focusing on his needs not only will increase the chances of getting him to listen to you, it will allow you to bask in the warm glow of altruism. He will appreciate your efforts and respond in kind. Below are some tips on how to express your feelings selflessly, getting the same points across without looking like a pig.

Selfless Subjects for Discussion

- ♥ What is wrong with you
- ♥ Why you are the way you are
- ♥ What's wrong with the way you are

The Truth of the Matter

A poet once wrote, "Beauty is truth, truth beauty,—that is all / Ye know on earth, and all ye need to know." Is truth really beauty? Is it really all ye need to know? What if ye need to know something else, like where the car keys are? Also, does this mean that truth is only skin-deep? That it is as it does? The truth is, the truth is no more beautiful than any other thing you might say to each other in the middle of an argument. Before going after it, ask yourself:

How ugly is the truth?

Truth	Attractiveness Level
I'm worried about how we're getting along.	Plain
I don't think we get along very well.	Homely
It's impossible to get along with you.	Unsightly
No one will ever get along with you.	Hideous
No one will ever love you.	Fugly

When the demise of a relationship is blamed on "lack of communication," you can be sure that there was plenty of it, just the wrong kind. While most communication involves words, it is also possible to communicate without them. In fact, most couples do the better part of their communicating in silence, and save the words for last.

Nonverbal Types of Communication

- ♥ Eye rolling
- ♥ Snorting
- ♥ Fake laughter or chuckling
- ♥ Driving like a maniac
- ♥ Banging around in the kitchen
- ♥ Unrepentant flatulence
- ♥ Falling asleep by nine

Despite the strides that have been made in the field of relationship communication, exchanges of this nature have a tendency to disappoint. While communication has its advantages, it's important not to place unreasonable expectations on the outcome. The possible outcomes of communication are limited and rarely enjoyable. These include:

1. Pouting
2. Tears
3. Hysteria

Pouting: A Succinct Way to Get Your Point Across

People often ask, "What if I want to make my displeasure clear, but I don't have the time to get into a full-blown argument?"

Good question. It is possible to distill several hours' worth of discussion into a single, gemlike gesture. These days, few of us have the time to go into it, and yet are loath to let our disappointment go by unexpressed.

Pouting can also be useful when you feel like something is wrong, but you can't quite put your feelings into words. The skilled pouter knows this, and finds that it is easier and altogether more effective to announce her discontentment silently than to attempt to fashion an airtight line of reasoning on the spot. The simple fact is, you don't know what's wrong. You just feel . . . It's just that you . . . I mean, sometimes, you think . . . Forget it.

Finally, a good, long, petulant pout is the ideal mode of expression for the passive-aggressive conflict avoider. There is nothing wrong with indulging your approach-avoidance personality disorder once in a while, when you feel like it. So, remember, when in doubt, say it with your lower lip.

Why Cry? Toward a
Science of Lachrymosity

Recent years have seen an explosion of work in the sciences and humanities on science's last great frontier: the Problem of Weeping. Despite a lively, ongoing interest in what's the matter now, the question of what causes tearful behavior in humans remains largely unanswered. Why do people spring leaks? Will they necessarily feel better after they let it all out? What exactly is a "good" cry, and how does it differ from a not-so-good one? Can there be a scientific theory of sniveling? If so, what form should this theory take? Should it necessarily be tear-shaped? Or could a pear shape pass? If not, why not, exactly?

This year, the National Center for Plangent Behavior will draw together researchers from all areas in an interdisciplinary exploration of sobbing uncontrollably to host the First Annual Conference dedicated to these and other questions.

CONFERENCE SCHEDULE AND ABSTRACTS

Introduction to Sniffling

Dr. Helen Gladstone, Ph.D.

The aim of this workshop is to provide an introduction to the theory of the emotional flesh wound and explore its relevance to postnasal drip. There will be three sections, each consisting of a lecture, interspersed with group and individual exercises. Facial tissue will be provided.

Part 1. Introduction to Slight Injuries and Their Effluent Effects. In this workshop, we will explore the miasmic response to the infelicitous remark, whether deliberate or unintended. Why do some comments elicit sarcastic responses, while others produce facial moistening? Why are you so sensitive?

Part 2. That Smarts!: The Emotional Flesh Wound and Its Relation to Spontaneous Effluvia. Is there such a thing as an archetypal insult? Is it all a matter of perception? Must it be intentional to be wounding? Also covered: Rejecting Kleenex, or The Johnsonian and Johnsonian Objection (Scott, 1983).

Part 3. "I Said I Wasn't Mad!": The Two Faces of Hurt. How come sometimes people say they are not crying when they really are? Are they crazy? In recent years, at least three new theories have been proposed to address this question: McNulty's implausible denial theory, Petrocelli's hard-luck-story model, and Wiggins's theory of the totally unreliable other. Also explored, why are tears so salty?

Dr. Helen Gladstone, Ph.D., author of Cry Me a River, My Kayak Is Stuck, *is a writer and lecturer living in Massapequa, New York.*

From Teardrops to Phlegm: Toward a Re-Contextualization of Blubbering

Rodney Yu and Felicity Shank

Is it polite to tear up at work? Would sobbing quietly in my cubicle be acceptable? What if something comes flying out of my nose? Should I make sure that someone is present when I tear up anyway, just in case my ducts clog? My lips are aquiver, is this normal? When is mucus appropriate? Moral and legal responsibility? Free will?

Despite modern advances, the problem of where and how openly to weep remains poorly characterized in the framework of the social sciences. Many agree that crying is a real phenomenon that correlates to a sudden marked decline in cheerfulness, yet it is notoriously hard to understand how such a complex phenomenon should escalate and whether it should occur in a social environment at all. These and other issues will be explored in depth.

Doctors Rodney Yu and Felicity Shank head the Department of Puling at the Plaintive Research Institute. They are currently developing a new quiz show titled NOW What's Wrong? for Lifetime Television.

Hysteria: The Great Equalizer

There is no other type of relationship in which we feel as safe, understood, or accepted as in a love relationship, which is why we are not afraid to be at our worst in front of lovers. Not since we were toddlers pitching tantrums for Mom and Dad have most of us felt this free to express our resentment, bitterness, and rage. Once you've opened up the floodgates of communication, there is often nowhere to go but completely off the handle. This is normal. In fact, quite often, it is the reason that communication was opened in the first place. When sex has cooled, hysteria is a great way for both of you to get in touch with the animal in you.

Experts agree that it is healthy to express your anger, and healthiest to express your anger with someone whose reaction to your anger you can predict. Becoming hysterical with strangers, especially those not familiar with your customs, can be hazardous. On the flip side, there are times when hysterical outbursts *should* be reserved for strangers, especially unsuspecting telemarketers and directory assistance operators. These are a perfectly safe outlet for your anger, and are unlikely to track you down given their notorious ineptitude at getting your or for that matter anyone's name, number, or address right.

If, after years of earsplitting disagreements, you are starting to toy with the idea of separation, but are not sure if, ultimately, this is what you want, pitching a fit is a great way to test your own courage and commitment to the idea of saying adiós. Do you have the guts, the follow-through, the where-withal? Will you really go through with it this time? Try saying something awful and permanent sounding. See how your partner responds. Then watch for subtle clues, like packing.

When All Else Fails:
Getting to "Fuck You"

In the old days, breaking up was a fairly straightforward exercise involving, simply, leaving. Today, when so many couples find themselves inhabiting different apartments, cities, and states of mind, "leaving" is not the clear-cut action it once was.

For past generations, dissolving a partnership was often a legal matter, involving other people, property, and children. More often than not, the services of lawyers, movers, and slutty secretaries were required to make a separation official. Our parents also had the right tools at their disposal. Most of them waited until a deep-seated hatred for each other had set in before bringing out the big guns like "divorce." Today, our guns are smaller and fuzzier. Those of us who are not married find we occasionally bring them out just to wave around for a bit, maybe to pistol-whip someone, but rarely to shoot. Nothing is more embarrassing than tossing out an empty threat only to have it be taken seriously.

Nobody knows exactly why breaking up has become a protracted power struggle, although theories abound. One theory has it that it is difficult to sever ties when you can't seem to locate them in the first place. In many ways, it is similar to sitting around waiting for the phone to ring so you can decline to answer it. Others favor the no-fault hypothesis, wherein couples become so entrenched in their right to be right that they refuse to give the other the satisfaction of being wronged.

One thing is known for sure, breaking up is hard to do. In fact, it is so hard that many people find themselves trying and failing to pry themselves loose from their significant others time and time again. For most modern couples, it's never really over on the first try. It often takes at least five to get it right. This can lead to confusion. You may spend months of valuable time and effort turning your friends against your boyfriend only to discover that you can't live without him at the last minute. Family members and friends may find themselves in the awkward situation of despising a lover with whom you have just reunited. Your mother will have an especially hard time with this, as it is her job to be supportive of your decisions, no matter how stupid they are.

The Custody Problem

Chances are your union has not been blessed with offspring. This is good news for everyone involved. However, before you pop the buttons on your fly, be warned that this does not mean the two of you will not soon be embroiled in a protracted custody battle of another nature. I speak of the little matter of your friends.

Which ones are his? Which ones are yours? Which one did you think was yours until he started enlisting your ex as his new wingman at parties? Generally speaking, the rule is, you get to keep yours and he gets to keep his—unless his have decided they like you better, which, of course, is up to them. While the postbreakup splitting of friends often occurs along fairly predictable gender or seniority lines, there are some exceptions to the norm that can cause trouble down the line.

When contemplating a breakup, it's advisable to try and identify the wild cards in your group of mutual acquaintances in advance and plan accordingly. You would do well to emulate U.S. foreign policy on this point whenever possible. Befriend the friend of your enemy as well as the enemy of your friend, just in case he or she should come in handy later. Come to think of it, the current administration's policies toward domestic issues—especially sticky instances of corporate corruption perpetrated by erstwhile good buddies—should come in handy in this matter as well. Should one of your friends go over to the other side postbreakup, simply do as our leaders do and bad-mouth said friend diligently in public, all the while pretending never to have met in person before. You can pay them back what you owe them later, when they come over for dinner.

Couple friends can be especially tricky, especially if the two of you introduced them. If the joining together of friends in holy matrimony is ever a good idea, it's certain to become problematic after you and your mate go your separate ways. You might want to dig around to see if you can foment some domestic discord over at their place, as a bitter split should obviate the allegiance issue down the line. If trying to rend other couples asunder is not an option for you (pussy), you'll want to make sure you win them both over to your side well in advance of your big day. Plant the seeds early, and watch them sprout into the proud, sturdy oak of their loyalty by the time you're ready to hit the road.

Favorite venues can also become the subject of heated custody battles. If you cannot convince your ex to leave town after your breakup, at least work out a schedule. Your favorite bars, restaurants, bookstores, and major metropolitan areas are not places you'll want to run into your ex and "a friend." This goes double if you happen to be with "a friend" of your own, especially if your "friend" actually happens to *be* a friend, or if the "friend" on your ex's arm is a "friend" of yours. This goes triple if your ex's "friend" is a "friend" of your "friend," at which point it all becomes terribly confusing.

Finally, and perhaps most important, there is the issue of who gets to keep ideas, opinions, pet peeves, expressions, jokes, and trademark phrases the two of you shared while together. You'd be surprised at how many exes will try to abscond with your intellectual property. Remember, it is these little nuggets of selfhood that make you who you are—

particularly now that you are without a boyfriend and quite possibly also lacking in the career, money, success, fame, and attractiveness departments. The last thing you want is your own jokes, catchphrases, and observations handed back to you by an unsuspecting third party who "always thought [your ex] was so funny." Amusing as your jokes might have been when you first thought of them, they will not sound the least bit funny in this context. Do yourself a favor and nip the copyright infringement in the bud before it is too late. You might try serving him with official-looking papers. Just make sure you don't pick a "friend" who "always thought he was so funny" to deliver them. Next thing you know you'll be running into them in your favorite bedroom.

Review: The Seven Phases of Love, or, What Just Happened?

Phase 1: Attraction Sprinkled with Anxiety

Couple feels first pangs of attraction. Attraction is the feeling that causes desire to take clothes off in the company of relatively unknown other. Anxiety is a natural offshoot of attraction, as nakedness is inherently embarrassing. Worst-case outcome: the person you are attracted to does not wish to get naked with you, leaving you naked by yourself. Best-case outcome: he does want to get naked with you, leading to a host of other, more long-term problems.

Phase 2: Dating Laced with Irritation

Once a mutual attraction between two people has been established, couple may want to enter a situation in which sex is the natural outcome. Obviously, for sex to occur, two people must first find themselves in the same place at the same time—unless they count phone sex, preferred by partners who find themselves in different states, countries, time zones, or states of mind. Problems arise when partners find they are in different leagues.

Phase 3: Exclusivity Accented in Resentment

The relationship has progressed to the point where anxiety gives way to the bitterness of disappointed expectations. Outings stop and couple skips directly to the part where they hang around on the couch for a period of anywhere from nine weeks to five years, watching TV and intending not to marry. In many cases, a fair amount of drinking is involved. Bickering is also a favored activity. Drinking, eating, and bickering are a good way to pass the time between sex, which will become increasingly infrequent. Count on some weight gain during this period and invest in some versatile sweatpants.

Phase 4: Commitment Punctuated by Repugnance

Couples reach the commitment phase when it has become clear that their options are not unlimited. This can happen anywhere from the mid-twenties to the late thirties, as you are never too young to start worrying about being too old. When unavailable ex-boyfriends and married friends talk about how hard their single friends have it, assume they are warning you, personally, in some sort of secret code. They probably know something you don't about your chances of finding love again.

Phase 5: Cohabitation Soaked in Loathing

What separates married couples from couples who live together for years without ever splitting a checking account? It all comes down to sharing. When a couple decides to live together as a way to remain single while not remaining single, you can bet that they have no intention of forgetting which belongings are theirs. Books and CDs may share shelf space, but not before they are secretly labeled. Secret labeling is usually duly noted by not-stupid partner, who may begin to engage in such goodwill gestures as saving grocery bill receipts and buying personal milk supply. There is nothing like keeping track of you and your beloved's pasta consumption-to-purchasing ratio to keep the flames of resentment burning.

Phase 6: Separation Peppered by Longing

Do not be alarmed if, after a long acrimonious period, your ex–significant other suddenly acquires a patina of desirability unnoticed by you since the early days of your courtship. After the separation, your formerly repulsive partner will glow as if lighted from within with the incandescence of a thousand bulbs, like the MGM Grand.

Phase 7: Breakup Suffused in Everlasting Love

Bravely, the two of you decide to forge ahead with the decision to break up. Your partner's courage, decisiveness, and determination—heretofore not so much in evidence—will fuel feelings of admiration and respect long ago forgotten. Making the decision to end the relationship in low, rational tones, after months of screaming, will make you feel all grown up and civilized. You may even envision yourself having an occasional friendly dinner with your soon-to-be ex down the line, swapping urbane stories and sharing wry insights about love, life, and loss. How his eyes will twinkle and crinkle. Longing becomes more intense as partner is now seemingly unattainable and subsequently attractive again. Maybe you should have sex one more time for old times' sake. There's a good idea.

PART SEVEN

The Void

Getting Over It

We are living in dangerously repressive times. Slowly, stealthily, silently, every day, in every way, our civil liberties and personal freedoms are being eroded. There are those who would even control our innermost thoughts, feelings, and impulses in the name of a greater, common good. I speak, of course, of the twin tyrannies of "moving on" and "being cool," both of which are now the law.

In some circles, nothing is considered more hopelessly retrograde than not "moving on" immediately following a breakup. In fact, these days, it is considered very bad form not to remain friends with one's ex. But remaining friends with one's ex can be tricky, especially if the breakup has been an acrimonious one. One way to circumvent this problem is by continuing to sleep together after the breakup.

Having Sex with Your Ex

Having sex with your ex is a good way to remain friends with him. This is not nearly as unorthodox as it may seem at first glance, as remaining friends with your ex usually leads to sex anyway. Most freshly broken up couples find that in order to remain amicable, it's better not to say much. Lunch with your ex is a prelude to disaster, as time in between chewing would normally be filled with friendly conversation. It probably goes without saying that if the two of you had been capable of having a friendly lunch, you'd still be together today. Sex with your ex, on the other hand, allows the two of you to spend quality time together without bringing up problematic subjects—such as sex.

Having Sex with Your Friend and Telling Your Ex

A common pitfall of having sex with your now-friendly ex is that you may find yourself having to keep secrets from him that you don't normally keep from your friends. Many an interpersonal relation has been felled by the ax of over-sharing. Asking a recent ex about his love life is almost never advisable. Most couples find it hard to remain friends with their exes once their exes start having sex with people they know. However, if you were never entirely sold on the idea of remaining friends with your ex in the first place, describing new affairs to him in vivid detail will enable you to free yourself of his company while managing to appear innocent of unfriendliness.

Breaking Up with Your Ex (Again)

Once your ex has started sleeping with someone else, it is acceptable to stop being his friend again. Remember this, and use it to your advantage. Genially coax information about his latest exploits from your ex, making sure to claim friendship and to assume a "down with it" demeanor, then react with shock when he comes out with it. Deftly switch into ex-girlfriend mode, and beg out of future conversations on the grounds of "not being ready" for this yet. As long as you graciously promise to resume the friendship at a later date, you'll probably never have to.

Ten Ways to Feel Good
Between Relationships

You're no longer in a relationship. Whether you took off in a snit of anger, were dumped, or simply agreed to part ways because neither one of you could stand the sight of each other for one more day, the transition from being in a relationship to being alone is not an easy one. You've regretted the whole thing, told him so, slept with him, regretted that, told him so, and spent seventy-two hours in front of the TV, waiting for the phone to ring. Single life stretches before you like an endless desert. You break into tears at the sight of a fork. Now what?

1. Get Healthy

Many dysfunctional couples enjoy gaining weight together and then blaming each other for the resulting flab. Use a breakup as an opportunity to shed unwanted pounds the easy way. While being in a long-term relationship often results in the kind of gnawing, low-grade depression that can lead to eating a box of crackers while watching *Lou Dobbs Moneyline* for no reason other than one has lost one's will to change the channel, newly single people often find they are much too terrified to eat. If the relationship ended on a particularly ugly note, a period of spontaneous vomiting might help speed things up.

2. Smell the Fucking Roses

One of the few immediate advantages of a horrible breakup is the forty-eight-hour period of euphoria that follows. You will feel (after the vomiting lets up) that a boulder has been lifted from your shoulders. Also, a certain attendant giddiness should be present. These feelings are the natural result of dehydration and lack of sleep, but this does not mean they can't be enjoyed to the fullest. Turn on loud music and dance around. Try on all your clothes and visualize yourself on a series of fabulous dates. Attempt to visualize what a fabulous date would be like. Call all your friends and tell them about how fresh and full of possibility the world seems suddenly. Encourage them to dump their boyfriends. If they balk at the suggestion, imply that they are in denial. You're going to need a sidekick.

3. Dream Your Dreamy Little Dreams

Now that you've left the relationship, you naturally feel as though you might do anything. As long as you are still in that euphoric period, go ahead and dream about moving to a new city, getting a new job, finding a new apartment. While you're at it, imagine yourself as a rock star, a supermodel, or a normal, healthy, well-adjusted person. The sky's the limit.

4. Complain 'n' Blame

Avoid introspection, self-examination, or any type of behavior that could lead to feelings of guilt, self-doubt, or learning. Learning can be especially dangerous between relationships, as it could lead to concluding that the breakup was one's own fault. Not only is it too late for this realization to be of any use whatsoever, it could result in premature apologizing during the rebound.

5. Briefly Go Insane

There is no better time to lose one's marbles than in the period between a long-term relationship and a rebound. After the brief period of euphoria has subsided, many people find themselves at a loss as to what to do with their free time now that breaking up is no longer their full-time occupation. One way to channel all that excess energy and contentiousness is to turn it against oneself.

6. Alienate Your Family

As long as you're going to make it on your own, why not go whole hog? This is a time to dwell on everything everyone has ever done to you. Remember the time your mom wouldn't let you go see (insert age-appropriate teen sex movie title here) with your friends, and instead offered to take you herself and "explain" it to you? "Explain" to your mom in no uncertain terms that you've identified this particular childhood trauma as the root cause of all your recent relationship woes, and demand that she pay for your therapy.

7. Get Professional Help

Use the money to buy yourself a friend. Now that no one else is speaking to you, you're going to need it.

8. Eat Chocolate Donuts

Preferably in bed, with the TV on. Don't bother to brush teeth. Instead, think about how great it is to be an adult and have no one tell you what to do.

9. Be Impatient

While it may be true that all things come to those who wait, they come faster to those who charge the all-you-can-eat buffet table of life, nostrils flaring. Begin looking for your next relationship as soon as you have left your old one.

10. Plan Your Revenge

You may not be able to get him back, but you can get back at him. Every day, go inside yourself to that part of your mind that's mean-spirited and petty and ask it for the guidance to steer you to the right place. Listen for the answers. Have trouble hearing the answers because the part of yourself that's intuitive and wise won't shut up. Ask that part of yourself to steer you to a happier, more centered space of warmth and wisdom and goodwill. Once there, tell that part of yourself to go fuck itself.

Codepndent Some More!

Copious lip service is paid to the notion that the ideal relationship should be a concordant union, a state of harmonious two-ness in which the give and the take are meted out in equal proportion.

This is crazy talk. For one thing, there will be times when one of you gives shit and the other takes umbrage, throwing the entire give-take balance out of whack. Also, relationships are forged from passion, and passion has a tendency to get loud and trigger migraines. In other words, if what you want is harmony, you are shopping in the wrong aisle.

The only way to ensure an equal give-take ratio is for the give and the take to be transactional and distributed along strict power lines. If you are looking for *symbiosis,* you don't need love. You need:

1. a geisha
2. a hooker, or
3. a therapist

Surprised to find your therapist in such dubious company? Don't be. The days when the psychotherapist ruled supreme over the mental health profession are over, as most people nowadays would rather discuss their problems with an understanding pill. These days, it's probably safe to say that when he's not trying to talk you into coming to see him three times a week, your precious Dr. Nudelman is spending much of his time counseling the ferns.

Don't let this get you down on the doctor. It must get awfully lonely in that little room. And, career-wise, he's got his back against the wall. In fact, it may just be your turn to give something back, something besides $130 an hour. A little empathy would be nice. A short visit once in a while wouldn't kill you. Besides, now that you are single and obsessing on it hourly, your therapist might just turn out to be the friend you've been waiting for all these years: the friend who only wants to talk about you. One thing is abundantly clear: Dr. Nudelman needs you now more than ever.

But before taking the big step of placing your therapist squarely in the center of your life, it is advisable to rationally assess the relationship for what it is and what it's not. Remember that despite certain similarities—he never wants to *go* anywhere or *do* anything, he just wants to sit on the couch and talk about what's *wrong* with you, etc.—your therapist is *not* your boyfriend. For one thing, there will be no sex. For another, he will expect payment. Also, Dr. Nudelman probably wears terrible shoes.

Unfortunately, your relationship with your therapist is, alas, a relationship and therefore finite. At first, you will be thrilled by your therapist's awesome capacity for siding with you in every situation, but eventually, you will grow tired of it. Why is he always *implying* things about the guys you go out with? Why can't he ever take anything at face value? Why does he always assume that something is *wrong*? Why doesn't he ever talk about what *he* feels? Do we have to discuss every little thing you do in minute detail? Meanwhile Dr. Nudelman's look of empathetic concern never varies—not during your relationship, your breakup, your single period, your re-bound, or your next relationship. Things will go on like this for some time, until, sooner or later, you will realize that Dr. Nudelman is just a big asshole.

Which leads to a new problem. After all the years you've spent bickering, squabbling, and sulking in sullen silence together, it will not be easy to sever your relationship with your therapist. Now that Dr. Nudelman has found you, he will not let you go without a fight. Your problems have be-come his problems. Your neuroses are his ski vacation. You don't repeat old, destructive patterns, he don't eat. Yes, Dr. Nudelman has become codependent—and freeing yourself from his determined clutches may prove more difficult than you think.

Some tricks to try:

- Scour your local sex shop for the blow-up doll that most resembles you, and send it to your appointment, via mes-senger, in your place.
- At your next appointment, demand to know whether Dr. Nudelman entertained any inappropriate thoughts about the blow-up doll.
- Break down and confess your feelings of love for Dr. Nudelman, taking care to describe your ideal wedding in vivid detail.
- Tell Dr. Nudelman that you'd like to pay him, but that a lien has been placed on your piggy bank.
- Ask Dr. Nudelman if he'll accept hugs in lieu of payment.

If none of these methods work, simply refrain from mak-ing any more contact with your therapist. If necessary, change your phone number and consider relocation. Whatever you do, don't tell Dr. Nudelman in person that you have decided to leave. Pretend that everything is fine, then leave a message on his machine. Be kind, be gentle, be firm. And whatever you do for the next couple of days, don't pick up that phone. You don't want to hear what he has to say about you.

PART EIGHT

At Not Very
Long Last, Love

Why Wait? The Rebound

The closing stages of a long relationship can be protracted and painful. After months of emotional scrimmage and scuffle, a wise person will set aside a period of time for recovery. Then again a wise person will not normally get out much. If love is a drug, you're going to need something to take the edge off. Yes, when you're strung out on a breakup, a rebound is the hair of the dog that dumped you.

But what makes a rebound a rebound? In other words, what distinguishes a rebound from all the other ill-considered, poorly timed, and seat-of-the-pants sequential relationships you normally favor?

For one, rebound relationships are notable for their alarming proximity to previous relationships. Rebounders eschew the requisite waiting period between a breakup and a mad, new love, unreasonably taxing their friends with tales of woe immediately followed by tales of unseemly happiness and frequent sex. This is the primary reason why rebounds are discouraged and frowned upon. Just because you don't need a rest from your emotional roller-coaster ride doesn't mean your friends and family don't.

Another characteristic of rebounds is that they tend to proceed at a pace usually associated with bullet trains and F-15s. This is in part because they enjoy the momentum built up during the last relationship, and in part because rebounds have a limited life span, and rebounders try to make the most out of the situation while there's still time.

While it's true that for the genuine serial monogamist, every relationship is a rebound of sorts, some are more so than others. If you're not sure whether your most recent relationship counts as a rebound, ask yourself the following:

- Is your new boyfriend the polar opposite of your last boyfriend?
- Do you find yourself having to explain the advantages of your new boyfriend to friends?
- Do your friends stare at you blankly when you do?
- Do you find yourself making allowances for traits possessed by your new boyfriend that you have vociferously pooh-poohed in the past (e.g., vegetarianism, an overdependence on horoscopes, illiteracy)?
- Did you vow never to fall in love again within twenty-four hours of meeting your new boyfriend?
- Did you fervently deny any interest whatsoever in your new boyfriend within the twenty-four hours previous to falling in love with your new boyfriend?

Rebounds are not that hard to identify once you know what to look for. For example, Dennis Rodman was once recognized as one of the NBA's premier rebounders. Whether or not you know much about basketball, this probably wouldn't surprise you. For one thing, just look at him. He's the last thing you need right now. Then again, you have just survived a tragic breakup; wouldn't it be nice to feel wild and free and underdressed? Just don't get too involved.

Common Rebound Scenarios

The Scheduled Rebound

You know that squirrelly "friend" who's been waiting in the wings? The one who was always "there for you" whenever you "needed to talk" about your disintegrating relationship? Your friend understands the importance of laying the foundation before attempting to lay the pipe. On the bright side, there's no waiting involved. On the not-so-bright side, what a weasel.

The Recidivist Rebound

Also known as the comfort rebound, this is the preferred type of rebound of not very adventurous obsessive-compulsive types and petty criminals. There's a reason convenience stores are the frequent target of dim-witted perpetrators: they are easy to locate, predictably laid out, and open all night. If the same can be said for your thriving chain of former boyfriends, you're in business.

The Reactionary Rebound

The reactionary rebound often begins with heartfelt discussion of how to prevent the rebound from becoming one, which will only ensure that it will. Your head says no, sure, but your heart says give it to me. Once all the agonized "We shouldn't do this" discussions have played themselves out, however, the rebound will lose its bounce and eventually hit the floor with a thud and stay there.

The Revenge Rebound

The least advisable of all forms of rebounds, the revenge rebound usually has less to do with your new boyfriend than it does with your ex-boyfriend. For a revenge rebound to be really effective, your ex-boyfriend must not only be made aware of it, but also be given daily updates on its progress. Spare yourself the trouble and the grief. A rebound should be a restorative experience. Sharing your rebound with an ex-boyfriend who refuses to be jealous will only ruin it.

The Rebound Rebound

Also known as your next relationship.

Falling in Love Again

After years spent fighting to keep a relationship to-gether, months spent fighting to pull it apart, and weeks spent fighting over who gets to keep the couch, the sensation of being suddenly single can feel like a generous hit of nitrous oxide. You're floating! And, indeed, you are. With no significant other to weigh you down, or boss you around, or distract you with his mouth-breathing, you sud-denly feel as though you can do anything. At all! So you buy new curtains.

The buying of curtains, though it may not seem so at first glance, is an important first step in falling in love again. Cur-tains purchased alone are almost invariably more interesting than curtains purchased in tandem, for the very simple rea-son that their purchase does not require consensus. As a con-sequence, the curtains will probably not be white. In fact, they may not even be curtains. You may decide to festoon your windows with, say, strands of tinsel, or old gum wrap-pers, or cardboard, even. However you choose to block out the light, you will spend the first few days in your new apart-ment thinking to yourself, "Why did it never occur to me to hang a shower curtain from my bedroom window before? Look how the little gel-filled ducks throw curious colors on the walls! How the little frogs glow and dance! Life is indeed glorious." And then you will feel wild. Free. A little crazy. You will feel as if you have stumbled across a marvelous new invention, this "being alone." Who knew there would be so much closet space?

Emboldened by your new curtains, you will embark upon a rigorous regimen of self-improvement and self-discovery. You may purchase place mats, even pets. You almost certainly will draw up a variety of lists detailing a) the sort of person you plan to become, b) the sort of life this sort of person would lead, and c) the mistakes you plan never to repeat.

This will be your first mistake, as the making of such lists, though well intended, is misguided. In our self-help obsessed culture, we have been conditioned to look upon mistakes as something we should strive to eliminate from our lives. As usual, it is our culture that is sadly mistaken. Of all the things that make our lives what they are—our achievements, our successes, our joys, our sorrows, our friends, mayonnaise, whatever—it is our mistakes that make the most lasting impact. Nothing shapes a life like a series of really stupid moves. If rules are made to be broken, then mistakes are made to be repeated, because rule number one is, you don't repeat mistakes.

The very first mistake you are doomed to repeat is the vow to do things differently next time. Not only are you setting yourself up for failure and ensuring that the fall will be a nasty one, but you are leaving yourself wide open to the ridicule of others. How much collective face could be saved if people stopped running around squawking about everything they've "learned" and how much they've "grown." Unfortunately, most people start running around and doing exactly that the minute they've hung their new curtains. So commence the "Herewith, all lameness terminates," or H.A.L.T. talks, wherein you will gather your friends together and solemnly vow:

1. To remain single for at least a year and focus on your career.
2. To "date around" while remaining blithely uncommitted to any one person.
3. To avoid becoming obsessed with anyone you have just met.
4. To avoid—if obsession is inevitable—spending more than two days a week with the person you have just met.
5. To avoid talking to friends about said person more than twice a week.
6. To stop forwarding cute e-mails from above-mentioned person.
7. To steer clear of moving in together.
8. To hold on to your curtains at all cost.

But Exactly How Great Is He?
"Relate, Alienate, Evacuate"

There's nothing like falling instantly in love to make you want to tell everybody all about it. And there's nothing like telling everybody all about it to instantly clear a room.

While it is perfectly acceptable to announce to your friends that you have once again clambered aboard the love bus, please regale in moderation. Two to three weeks of blissed-out logorrhea is generally considered sufficient in most social circles. After that, you may start to wear out your welcome. If the euphoria does not subside within a reasonable amount of time, it might be advisable to curtail further displays of it. Try sneaking off and smothering yourself with a pillow in the next room before rejoining the party. Also, take a moment to get to know your audience. Are you talking to your grandmother? Your therapist? Your mom? If not, consider keeping it to yourself. Everybody is really happy for you, they're just not too thrilled at the prospect of making a career out of it.

If you haven't been talking too much, yet your friends look as though they have spent the last few hours in a tempest-tossed dinghy every time you open your mouth, you might want to take a close look at what you are sharing. Here are some subjects you might want to think about avoiding:

1. The Cute Things He Does

You are completely enthralled by your new boyfriend and all the little cute things he does. Yet no attempts at describing his funny jokes, his endearing quirks, or his poignant grooming habits will do him justice. Remember, your new boyfriend is your own personal little miracle. No one else can even remotely understand. They really can't. So give it a rest.

2. Feelings You Just Can't Describe

You are beset with emotions that words can't describe. If you're reasonably sure that what you are feeling is indescribable, accept it graciously and move on to other, describable subjects. Attempts to describe the indescribable usually end in pointless blathering, glazed stares, and parties breaking up early.

3. His Enormous Penis

Though everybody enjoys a good genital chat now and again, it is possible for the newly enamored person to get a little carried away. While a clinical comparison of characteristics is always enlightening, nobody wants to hear the word "huge" more than once an hour. Mention it once, then read the reaction in the room. Frequent, too-ardent endorsements can begin to sound like a challenge. The last thing you want is for your friends to start feeling like they have to defend their boyfriends' honor. The whole thing can get competitive and ugly.

4. Happiness

It's great that you're happy. Everybody is happy that you're happy. Everyone is happy to be happy that you're happy. Realize this, then realize that everyone will be happier when you stop derailing the conversational train, tragically killing every other topic on board. Remember, everybody is happy, happy, happy for you, but mainly, they are waiting patiently for your life to return to normal so they can start talking about your problems again.

You were a lot more fun to be around when you were crazy.

Acknowledgments

Special thanks to my editor Janelle Duryea, without whom this book would not have been possible, because it was her idea. She made me do it, nurtured it, and then took off to do something more "noble" with her life. I hope she's happy. Thanks to Katie Zug, my second editor, for taking in a little orphaned manuscript and beating it into shape, and to my agent, Gary Morris, for his encouragement and support. Extra-special thanks to my mom, Olga Penny, my sister, Magaly Chocano, my brother, Gonzalo Chocano, and my friend Heather Havrilesky for reading the manuscript more times than was healthy for them, and for their many long-distance pep talks. Sorry about the phone bills.

About the Author

CARINA CHOCANO writes for Salon.com. Her work has also appeared in *The New Yorker* and *Bust* magazine. She lives in Los Angeles.